The Perfectly Painted Picture

Mildred Juanita Hart

© Mildred Juanita Hart
2014 Kingdom Builders Publications

All rights reserved. No part of this book may be reproduced or transmitted in any form or by any means without written permission from the author.

Printed in the USA

ISBN 978-0-578-15487-9

Library of Congress Control Number 2014958505

Authored by
Mildred Juanita Hart

Editor
Batina L. Dawson

Photograph
Anitra Bell Hart
John F. Hart, Sr.

THE PERFECTLY PAINTED PICTURE

DEDICATION

In memory of my mother, Mrs. Naomi M. McLeod, My mother-in-law, Mrs. Viola D. Farmer, My step-mother and friend, Mrs. Vernice B. Poole, You endured the storms of life with grace, faith, courage and tenacity.

ACKNOWLEDGMENTS

To *"Granny's Gang"* (my husband James, my children, Alfreta, Felicia, James, John, and Batina, along with their spouses, Anitra, Monica, and Sherman, and my grandchildren); you're precious jewels indeed. You're the wind in my sails. I'm blessed to have such a great cheering squad rooting for my team.

Reverend Roscoe Poole, Jr., my daddy, I'm truly grateful that God chose you to be my father. And Nell, I thank you as well. Sonya, I'm thankful for our special aunt/niece relationship. Sam, thanks for your respect and encouragement. And Lennon II, thank you for pressing.

To my siblings, extended family and friends who are too numerous to name individually, and I dare not leave any of you out, I appreciate each unique gift that you add to the mix. You're the butter, eggs, sugar, and flavor in my cake. We're family by design.

To Williams Chapel Church family, I thank all of you so very much for your love, support, encouragement, prayers, and listening ears.

CONTENTS

DEDICATION .... **IV**
ACKNOWLEDGMENTS .... **V**
CONTENTS **6**
AUTHOR'S NOTES **8**
    LIFE AND ART 9
    EMERGING FROM THE CHAOS 10
    PROLOGUE 13
    THE PERFECTLY PAINTED PICTURE 19
CHAPTER ONE **20**
    RELATIONSHIPS 25
CHAPTER TWO **26**
CHAPTER THREE **29**
    ESCAPE CLAUSE 33
CHAPTER FOUR **35**
    I DON'T WANT TO GO THERE ANYMORE 38
CHAPTER FIVE **39**
    BROTHERS 42
CHAPTER SIX **45**
    SPECULUM 47
CHAPTER SEVEN **48**
    LIFE GOES ON 52
CHAPTER EIGHT **53**
    CRISIS 55
CHAPTER NINE **56**
CHAPTER TEN **58**
    HAND AND HEART 60
CHAPTER ELEVEN **61**
    YOU WERE THERE 65
CHAPTER TWELVE **67**
    LOVE AND FORGIVENESS 72
CHAPTER THIRTEEN **75**
    A WORD PLAY ON LIFE 81
CHAPTER FOURTEEN **83**

LETTING GO	88
CHAPTER FIFTEEN	**89**
I HAVE BEEN THERE TOO!	92
CHAPTER SIXTEEN	**94**
TAKE ME HIGHER	98
PRAYER	99
EPILOGUE	102
PEACE	105
ANOTHER STROKE OF THE BRUSH	107
DOING THE RIGHT THING THE HARD WAY	108
ABOUT THE AUTHOR	**ERROR! BOOKMARK NOT DEFINED.**

AUTHOR'S NOTES

"**THE PERFECTLY PAINTED PICTURE**" is a fictitious work based on spiritual truths and the human experience. The names, characters, incidents, even the animals are imaginative.

The purpose of this book is to vividly depict real life through figurative representations and imagined occurrences, but above all, to represent Christ, His love and forgiveness. As you journey down the pathways of life with me and the characters on these pages, perhaps, you might recognize yourself or others. Pray. And remember, the very same love, hope, peace, and joy found in the Gospels are extended and available to each and every partaker on this journey called, "life". My prayer is, "Whenever and wherever this narrative find and connect with you, it'll bring enjoyment, enlightenment, empowerment, emancipation, elevation and entertainment".

Thank you for taking the time out of your busy schedules and lives to purchase, read, and/or share these writings. I truly appreciate it. It's my belief, through the story, the poetry, and the purpose, you'll be blessed.

I believe in "Divine Inspiration". First and foremost, these words have reached, touched, and ministered to some areas in my own life. Though I'm expounding this message as a lay person, nevertheless, *I know* that it's for the ministry of edification and exhortation. I also believe that God has chosen me, in this season, for this. I am humbled even the more because I understand and acknowledge that it's for His Glory!

LIFE AND ART

Perfected or Imperfect;
Compassionate or indifferent;
Like life, art is a continuous cycle.

As long as there's breath and imagination,
Dreams and visions,
Depth and length,
Hope and possibilities,
Appreciation and commitment,
Expectation and responsibility;
There will be amazement, fulfillment, beauty, growth,
accomplishment, benefits and provisions.

Life and art
Art and life

With every stroke of the brush and the pen;
With every tap of the chisel and focus of the lens;
With every note played and every lyric sung,
The cycle continues on endlessly.

Art imitating life
Life imitating art

EMERGING FROM THE CHAOS

Emerging from the chaos with residue sticking like glue,
and feeling worse for wear.
Issues that oftentimes become weaknesses,
but sometimes strengths.
Issues that don't necessarily belong to me,
Issues passed down like a family inheritance,
or second-hand clothes,
nevertheless, have hitched-hiked a ride upon my back,
staked out their claim and took up residence,
unbeknownst to me, they really sought ownership.

They didn't ask permission or wait for an invitation,
make reservations or inquire about a vacancy,
nor did they care that I was otherwise occupied.
Still, I will not become their victim,

The more these things prey upon me,
The harder I push,
The more I search for a way out.
They will not define, dominate, or dictate to me,
Nor will I let them impede my future, my destiny.

Through discouragement and distress,
Entanglement and agitation,
Dysfunction and malfunction,
Dissatisfaction and affliction,

THE PERFECTLY PAINTED PICTURE

I pushed.
Pushing until, discontentment turned into contentment
Pushing until, being called a "survivor" sounded like victory,
Still, pushing even beyond that.

Sometimes, to survive simply means:
The thing didn't kill you though it tried,
You just got by or barely escaped.

I saw no justice in that!
When my aim is to overcome,
And live a victorious life!
I'm in it to win it, from start to finish,
But I know that it will take Someone greater than I.
His name is Jesus Christ!
With great resolve, I called on Him.
His peace and rest reached a place deep inside of me:
Unfamiliar, unacquainted, and unchartered territory.
Strangely, I did not recognize myself.
For there were parts of me that I had never given up:
Parts that I had built an encampment around.
I had no comprehension of this newfound tranquility,
And I knew, at that moment, I wanted more.
So I continued to push,
Push until, I was thrust forward,
out of my familiar environment like a babe pushed from the womb.
Emerging from the struggle to become who I was really meant to be,

Separated from the place and the things that incubated,
Protected, molded, and at times, stifled me,

The place in which I had become attached by the discords of life,
The place was all I knew,
It had become my comfort zone of sorts,
Nonetheless, my detachment was of great necessity.

Even if it meant going through long hours of travail, and trauma,
And life altering conditions,
Emerge I must from the chaos that was determined to destroy me from within!
Chipping constantly at my inner core:
Who I am,
What I know,
What I hope to become.
Who God had created and purposed me to be.
So, in spite of the challenges and the changes ahead, I push!
I push until, the chaos is behind me!
I push until, I'm delivered!
I push until, I'm free!

PROLOGUE

What is the It?

In our lives, circumstances arise. They may be a conglomeration of many things: unresolved issues, denial, present day battles, etc. The situation can become volatile when combined with fear, failure, pride, stubbornness, unforgiveness, illness, grief, financial woes, and etc.

Presently, a vast number of people in our society face joblessness. We struggle through a dwindling job market though we have a willing work force. This plight doesn't just affect the jobless population. It is far reaching. The employer, the employee and his/her household, the community, the marketplace, and even the church have been affected; whereby, the church is an extension of the community.

The concerns associated with such a wide spread condition reaches beyond empty brick and mortar buildings, foreclosed homes, lost benefits, and repossessed cars. We also must come face to face with homelessness, hunger, exhausted unemployment funds, and scarce job prospects. However, this list only skims the top of the issue. Yet, they influence our bottom line on a daily basis whether the effect upon us is direct or indirect.

Through no fault of their own, innumerous employees from many levels within the work force find themselves without a job. Employers have to figuratively bite the bullet during times of economic upheaval. Loyal, long term workers as well as short term slackers get the ax. The just and the unjust bear the brunt together.

Whether we view the situation from the position of benefactor or beneficiary, none of us are left out of the equation. It's such an enormous problem; all of us in varying degrees are involved. If we're not bogged down in the muck and mire, we're exposed to the residuals.

Sometimes, we equate who we are with what we do, or our ability to maintain and/or possess. Regrettably, we value or devalue ourselves and others based on status, achievements, affluence, address, education, family pedigree, etc.

Oftentimes, when our lives appear to be in a state of chaos, we tend to lose our focus. We may shift from a state of being proactive to reactive, to retroactive. Seemingly, another problem will invite itself in before the last one exit. At other times, we may get caught up in a state of manageable chaos: tough, but not impossible times. Thankfully, most often, we are able to see pass the difficulties to a place of endurance, resolution, and peace.

Life contains so many variables. At best, we can set goals, make plans, make right choices, still, at some point in our lives, we're privy to those universal and very much human conditions stated in Ecclesiastes, Chapter Three concerning time.

Hopefully, we have a good grasp on life, but are not holding on so firmly that a shift will cause us to become disjointed. Life is filled with choices, challenges, risks, deviations, defeats, and victories.

In sports, no one plays to tie the game. Both sides play hard and they play to win. However, one team must lose. Once a victor has been declared, without knowing anything about the game, you can point out the defeated.

When we put our all into a thing our expectation is to prevail. After a defeat, the team or its' individual players doesn't toss their helmets, bats, balls, and/or clubs into a corner, and vow never to play again. Back in the locker room, the triumphant team can't afford to rest on its' laurels. There will be another day, more reviews and practices, another competition, more trials and errors. Though the team may be full of heart, hope, effort, and successes, it knows, there are still no guarantees.

The plays that were effective against one team may not necessarily work against another. Therefore, the coaches and the team have to be willing to shift: Players have to be alternated. There may have to be a variation of a play. In order to come out victorious, there may have to be a deviation to a practiced formation. The coach doesn't wait until the game is over to give the team a pep talk. Most likely, by half time, they have a fairly good prospective on how he/she views their performance.

Wind doesn't blow in the same direction all the time; it shifts. We must be willing to change also. We cannot use the same blueprints and expect to produce a different design.

As much as we would like to think otherwise, we never had control of our lives. We have the freedom to make our own choices, and to suffer our own consequences. We may try to manage our lives, but we can't control them.

God is real! Jesus is alive! The Holy Spirit rest, rules, and abides on the inside of me! This is my truth. It's my foundation. It's my guarantee. Any and everything else is subject to change.

God in His written Word has taught me that many afflictions will come. Trials, tests, and tribulations will present themselves. I am encouraged by His promise that He will never leave nor will He ever forsake me. When circumstances arise and try to overtake me, He will make a way of escape.

I love the Lord, and I know that He loves me, but that doesn't give me a free pass. He has also stated in His Word that it rains on the just as well as the unjust. At one time or another, all of us go through.

Like David, I know wherever I am, He is with me. There is no valley so low, no mountain so high that He cannot reach. With Jesus on my side, being hopeless is not an option. Hardships, trouble, disappointments, grief, and illness are more than just familiar terms to me. I am well acquainted with them. Quite honestly, going through is much more than just a walk or a run in the park. It's very often slow, long and painful. Jesus is able to sustain us in and during the process. Afterwards, we can view them as life experiences, teaching tools, testimonies, as well as strength, faith and stamina builders.

Whenever we go through, we don't have to go through alone. We oftentimes, pull or carry others into our struggles both intentionally and unintentionally. Some of us welcome and embrace someone to walk hand in hand with during the storms of life. We acknowledge our desire and need for comradeship. It is essential to our well-being that we have someone to commiserate with.

While some are drawn into our quandary voluntarily, others may get involuntarily drafted in. Unfortunately, some comrades may only want participants in or spectators to their pity party. Misery may love an audience, but the audience seldom enjoys the misery.

However, if you're invited to be a comrade, be a true and loyal one. When others entrust us with their innermost, heartfelt, intimate concerns we shouldn't take the invitation lightly or for granted or squander the trust advanced to us. I view trust as a precious treasure that has been acquired or loaned. If for whatever reason that treasure is misused, the giver will confiscate it. Usually, a trust once, twice or sometimes thrice wounded is kept close to the breast of the offended. It becomes difficult to relinquish that precious treasure again.

Misused trust victimizes already wounded warriors. They're distracted from the real battle by the friendly fire. Those who they assumed to be comrades turn out to be the enemy as well. In a real sense, these are the worst kinds of wounds. At least a warrior is aware of the presence and the agenda of the enemy. His goal is to kill, to steal, and to destroy by any means necessary. We don't expect loyalty, integrity, trustworthiness, or fair-mindedness to flow out of his camp. Destruction is his only rule, his only plan. Therefore, it's devastating when these types of behaviors and activities abound within our own camp.

In many instances, our dilemmas already make us feel as if we're isolated. We may feel picked on and picked apart. It's unhealthy and unwise to try to live in disconnect as opposed to relationship. A trustworthy comrade is out there. We have to believe and allow ourselves an open door. The hinges are constructed so that the door swings inwardly and outwardly. Sure it's a risk. Life in itself is a risky business. Somewhere, there stands a beacon on a hill or a magnificent light at the end of a dark and lonely tunnel. We may believe that our island insulates us, but it can become a prison as well.

In the pictures where Jesus is standing, knocking at the door, there is no door knob on the outer side. He cannot gain access unless we open up the door and let Him in. Jesus is a True and Faithful Friend. Trust Him. He wills to fellowship with us in spirit and in truth. He's also more than able to supply all of our needs and to give us an abundant life.

We need physical (person to person), emotional (self-awareness), spiritual (God-connected) relationships. It is about our wellness, our wholeness, our ability to give and to receive.

Just as the conception of our issues may be a result of numerous things, the resolution of those things may not involve one, but instead, a variety of things.

We may expect the answer(s) to our issues to come wrapped in a lovely, special delivery package, but it seldom does. We should be very careful that we don't miss our blessings because the outside appearance doesn't conform to our perception of what a blessing should look like.

In conclusion, trouble comes in many forms, shapes, sizes and intensities. Beware when you fall into divers' circumstances, isolating yourself, thinking you're the only one. None of us can live above the fray. Sooner or later, we will have an up close and personal encounter with trouble. We will not escape every confrontation. Life and time and chance happen to us all. When trouble comes, it won't be polite or a gentleman or knock on the door. It usually bombards its' way in, unannounced.

Nevertheless, the question remains, Will we become counteractive or allow trouble free access and free reign into our lives, into our homes, into our hearts and minds?

THE PERFECTLY PAINTED PICTURE

The picture captured my attention immediately.
It, himself could've posed for the portrait.
The painting appeared to be an exact likeness:
Those eyes, the ears that stood up straight and alert, that stubby tail,
Even the color of the mongrel's mane fit him to a tee.

It probably never would've won a contest based solely on beauty.
As his name implies, he definitely couldn't have placed as a thoroughbred.
Undoubtedly, no one would've ever expected such a homely dog to come from majestic lineage.
Yet, if he had been judged on his love and loyalty,
It would've been a formidable opponent.
Most assuredly, he would've come out on top.

Some may view the portrait and ask,
"Why would anyone waste precious time, and effort painting that uncomely creature?"
The Perfectly Painted Picture portrayed more than the canine's less than exceptional features.
Like It, his beauty came from a much deeper place.

Grandma often proclaimed that this, that or the other was a,
"Blessing in disguise".
Well, our blessing came to us in the form of a very unkempt dog.
It grew on us until all we saw was a friend.
From his first day with us, to his last, he was indeed a blessing.
In his own special way, It helped to change our lives.
And I'm so glad we opened our hearts to him.

CHAPTER ONE

When people visit us, they seldom understand why we have a picture of such an unusual looking mutt hanging in our foyer to greet them. Nevertheless, they often comment on how nice the frame is that incases the picture. I sometimes explain and at other times do not. More often, I just say, "That's a portrait of my dog, It".

About eight months after we were married, Gerald and I were strolling through the flea market. We weren't really looking for anything in particular. We were out enjoying the weather and one another. That's when I first saw the painting.

"That's It!" I told Gerald, pointing at the picture.

"That's what?" He asked.

"That looks just like my dog, It." I explained.

"Baby, do you want to buy this? He asked, his brows asking another question. "Why?"

"No. I was just saying, 'the dog in the painting resembles It'." I said hesitatingly.

"Are you sure?" He asked.

"Yes. Let's go." I said, taking hold of his hand again.

I refused to take another glimpse, but I wanted to. The picture was a reminder of some of the most favorable times in my childhood. It loved my brother, Alex and I unconditionally. He had a just because kind of love. We didn't have to do anything to earn his love except be ourselves.

Gerald knew about It. Still, I wondered if my husband fully appreciated the dog's significance to us. I didn't have to wonder for long, four months later to be exact.

On our first anniversary, I acquired another level of

enlightenment and assurance that our marriage was indeed meant to be. I knew that I loved my husband for all of the obvious reasons: He was a good man. He was kind, thoughtful, gentle, etc. But, I became very cognizant of the special gift God had given me when He sent Gerald into my life. I began to appreciate him over, above and beyond all of those easily come to mind adjectives. I loved my husband then. I love him today far more than words could ever define or communicate. But on that day, I understood that we were connected in a way I hadn't completely grasped before.

The portrait was more than Gerald giving simply because I wanted, needed, liked or requested something. For me, the painting represented security. I could trust him with my pain. He was secure in himself and strong enough to support me. He understood. He got It. With him, my heart was in a safe place. I could walk beside him in freedom and without fear.

I prayed to be the woman he needed me to be: his wife, his lover, his friend and someday, the mother of his children. I had learned that all of the love in the world could not and would not make or keep me happy if I wasn't happy with and within myself. Happiness is inner conditioning. Yet, the outward benefits it produces will help to gratify others.

I also realized that I had to make some difficult choices and be committed to working at them. In my opinion, you can't emerge from a storm without some residue.

Our first anniversary was on a chilly Saturday. Gerald was up early. He insisted on serving me breakfast in bed. My husband was overwhelming me with attention. And I loved it. I didn't want our fire to ever dwindle. I honored him, but unlike Sarah, I had not yet called him, "lord" though he had already proven himself to be the shepherd over our home.

The long stem roses were a surprise and so was the negligee. I could see that Gerald was being very attentive, but very affectionate as well. In giving the negligee, he had given me a "little" something for *himself*.

Quite frankly, my gift to him, Natural Elements served the same purpose. I loved that scent on him. It was as if I could breathe him into me. The combination of him and the cologne caused me to feel the earth, the wind, and the fire in him. It stirred something so sensual, so intimate, so natural and so very much ours and ours alone to share.

The biggest surprise of all was what I saw staring at me when I finally ventured out of our bedroom. Hanging in the foyer, where it still hangs today was the picture. Gerald had reframed it in a beautiful golden frame.

To me, at that moment, it was the most beautiful picture in the world. It would never be just a portrait of a homely little mutt, but a perfectly painted picture of something that wasn't so perfect and not held as special or significant by all. Nonetheless, It was so very precious in my sight.

Its' beauty was in the eyes of those who could or would allow themselves to take a deeper look. Its' beauty was much like our lives, much deeper than the superficial or surface things; far more than things that can change in a moment or can come and go with the tide. It was a symbol of all that was right in a world where so many things seemed to go wrong.

My emotions began to run amuck. I felt jubilation and sorrow along with every emotion in between: Joy for the happy times and the restoration that eventually took place in our family; heart ache for those things that had been lost forever; sorrow for the wasted time and effort spent on the unnecessary when we could've spent it on, "I love yous".

Today, the portrait is a symbol of the love, the hope, and the oneness we share in life in spite of its imperfections. It's also a reminder to me not to take the little, but special things for granted and not to allow the big things to overtake me.

Every now and then I have to think back, momentarily, in order to remind myself that life is not always how we see it. There are rarely, if ever any perfectly painted picture lives. All of us, at one time or another have or will experience our share of lumps, bumps and bruises. However, I've learned, it is how we choose to view them as well as what we choose to sustain us that will help to determine whether we overcome or succumb.

As my Grandma would often say, "Baby, you got to have a Safe Shelter, a Strong Tower. In times of storm, not every forlorn city crumples neither does every thriving city stand. Storms don't pick and choose who they'll fall down upon. Sooner or later, a storm or two will come to where all of us lay our heads. It's not a question of whether we've earned or deserve it or not. Honey, all we got to do is, keep on living.

"Believe me child, storms don't play favorites. The upright man and the crooked man's gardens both get watered during a good rain. And both of them are subject to the same ill winds. If you don't want to crumple, if you want to remain, you best have yourself a sure Hiding Place."

RELATIONSHIPS

Respect
  Embraces
    Love
      Appreciation
        Thankfulness
         Intimacy
          Oneness
           Nurturing
            Safety
             Honor
              Integrity
               Peace
                Sacred

RELATIVE, REDEFINING, RESPONSIBLE, REAFFIRMING, REWARDING, RESOURCEFUL, RESILILENT, RENDERING

CHAPTER TWO

"Ma! Ma! Tell Marla to leave me alone!" Alex cried from the front yard.

I kept on chasing him certain that Mama would never hear. Her soaps were on. Seemingly, we didn't even exist until the last one went off. Usually, but lately, with or without her soaps, Mama had entered into her own little world and shut us out. It appeared to us, we didn't have to be out of sight to be out of mind.

Much to my surprise and my regret, I heard, "Marla, bring your fast tail here! I'm tired of this fuss! I declare, you and Alex act like y'all are the devil's chirren for sure!"

I walked up to the porch dreading what I knew was coming next.

"Bop!" I heard when Mama's hand met the side of my head. My face stung and my ears rang, but I dared myself to cry knowing that her next words would be, "Gal, you best hush up before I give you something to cry for." And I had no doubt that she would too.

After glaring at me from eyes that could've melted butter, she said, "Now get back out yonder and play with your brother like you got some sense! Don't make me come to this door again! Do you hear me!

"Yes ma'am, Mama." I mumbled.

As soon as Mama had shut the door, Alex took off running, but I wasn't about to chase him. If Mama was in the mood to smack somebody else, I sure didn't want it to be me. She had never smacked me in my face before. She certainly hadn't called Alex or me, "the devil's chirren" before. I was growing sort of afraid of this new version of our mother. It's now apparent that

Mama no longer found any joy in being a wife, a mother or herself.

Closing my eyes, holding my arms out as if I was a bird in flight, I began to spin around until I became dizzy enough to open my eyes and see everything seemingly spinning around me: the trees, the clouds, everything. I was in my own little world then. Everybody and everything else, especially trouble was blocked out.

"Marla! Marla! Look! There it goes again. There's that dog again. I told you!" Alex yelled.

By the time I got my eyes fixed enough to see anything that wasn't twirling, the brown and white image was walking back into the woods.

What Alex had told me about the dog made me chase him in the first place which lead to Mama smacking me. So I felt, he was the one who deserved the lick.

Alex had told me that the dog was our Grandma coming back to keep an eye on us. I knew that it was just a dumb notion spoken by an even dumber boy. Regardless, I got angry or scared or both and chased him.

On one hand, the idea of Alex thinking our dear, sweet Grandma would show up in the form of a little sooner, a mere mutt made me angry enough to swat him a time or two if I could've caught him.

On the other hand, the idea of our dead Grandma showing back up as anything at all frightened me enough to give me goose pimples, but Alex would never know it. Although I knew he was just being his usual dumb self, I began to wonder if it could be possible.

    We missed Grandma terribly. We needed her even more. She seemed to have been the only one able to make sense of the craziness of life. She made us feel safe after life seemed to get too much for some: namely, Mama and Papa. Grandma could make things a little easier to take with just the sound of her voice.

Though I didn't desire for anyone else to feel the sadness or the loneliness or the helplessness I felt, still, I didn't understand why she had to be the one to go when there were so many others who could've gone in her place, Life nor death operates in that fashion despite my lack of comprehension about either. I was yet young with a lot more growing and even more learning to go.

I was beginning to understand one thing more clearly: Life really wasn't a perfectly painted picture. Instead, it's full of smears, eraser marks, coloring outside of the lines, along with things you can see, but can't understand a bit.

Even from young, inexperienced eyes, I saw that life was certainly anything but perfect. Nevertheless, some tended to put forth an awful lot of effort trying to present ours' that way before others who didn't have to live in the house with us.

For example, when Grandma got sick, it seemed as if people came from everywhere to see her, especially our fellow church members. Papa would turn into this real nice man, a man who had long departed from our house. He would pour on nice like he was pouring molasses over hot-buttered biscuits.

Before them, he was the perfect son, the perfect husband, the perfect father, the perfect Brother Wyatt. He was so polite, so welcoming, but it was just a facade. We knew, when the company was gone, that side of Papa was leaving with them.

CHAPTER THREE

The morning after we had first seen the dog, we were up early. We encountered more of Mama's hollering and more of Papa's walking out of the door, slamming it hard behind him without so much as a, "kiss my foot" before he got into his old, rusty truck and left for work.

Alex and I made a bee-line for our chores without being told. We could tell that Mama wasn't in any mood for anything nor was I in any mood to hear her calling us, "the devil's chirren" again or feeling her hand upside my head.

I had a pretty clear picture in my head of what the devil must look like on most days so I didn't appreciate people calling other people the devil, especially me or Alex, on any day. Alex may have been just a dumb, old boy, but he certainly wasn't any kin to the devil and neither was I.

Grandma used to say, "There ain't nothing beneath that ole slew-footed thang. Ain't nothing too bad for him to do. The badder it is, the better he likes it."

She didn't waste any time on the devil. Instead, she prayed hard, real hard against him until things got better. At times, I thought she was going to wear her knees clean out. I could tell without her uttering a single word when she had put down a good piece of praying the night before: As soon as I walked in her back door, the strong smell of liniment would hit me straight in the nose. I never doubted that somewhere in the midst of all of her prayers, she had called out my name a time or two; knowing that made me feel real good on the inside, even safe.

In my eyes, my grandma was not only the best grandma I

knew, she was also the best person I knew. She was the same wherever she went. Grandma always had an encouraging word, a piece of gingerbread, a 'just because' dime, and/or a big hug to give. She was a real nice lady. I never saw her handle anyone roughly. I never heard her speak to anyone harshly. She talked about the Lord a lot, a whole lot. And I believe Grandma loved Him just as much as she said.

I loved my Grandma. In a world that can oftentimes appear to be so cold, mean, distant and indifferent, she was like a graceful swan, swimming in calm waters. I believed with everything in me, mostly because I had seen it with my own eyes: When the waters turned turbulent which unfortunately had become the case around our house, she had the right touch and the right words to smooth things over again.

After her death, I tried to take on the task of fixing our fading family portrait. Countless times, I told myself that if I did more around the house, required less, I could fix whatever was ailing us. Then Papa wouldn't have anything to fuss about. Surely, that would make Mama cry less.

For all of my wanting, frustration and guilt appeared to be my only rewards. Seemingly, the more I tried to stay out of the way, the more I supposed I was in the way.

In retrospect, it is never the responsibility of the children to try to parent their parents. Children are incapable of such a monumental task. They aren't equipped in mind, body or spirit. Yet, due to various circumstances, far too often, children try to fill shoes that are much too large for their feet and/or try to wear hats that were never designed for their youthful heads. Notwithstanding, we try anyway.

I loved my mother and father, but it sure was hard to like their ways sometimes, most of the time. I told myself over and

THE PERFECTLY PAINTED PICTURE

over again that they just couldn't help themselves. Believing that was easier to take than believing they were the way they were on purpose.

Hurt had caused Papa to act the way he did. Hurt had caused Mama to react the way she did. And hurt pushed Alex and I in the middle, but offered us no relief or remedy. All of us were still a part of the picture, though we were now unrecognizable even to ourselves.

To me, Mama was more like a squawking hen who still sat on her nest, refusing to bulge even after her eggs hatched, afterwards, blaming her chicks for the consequences. She was no longer the even-tempered, gentle Mama she used to be. Instead, she had allowed deception to distort her perception of the circumstances of life and dictate her future outcome. Trouble seemed to have manipulated her into being its' puppet and she wasn't even trying to resist.

Likewise, Papa was folded, kneaded and twisted by forces from without and from within as if he were bread dough being prepared for the fiery furnace. Sometimes, he acted as if he'd been transformed into a raging bull or a fire-breathing dragon or both.

As a child, I never understood how one man could be so angry about so much? Oftentimes, I wondered if he took pleasure in reviving the same old hurts over and over and over again.

Little suited him anymore. Therefore, he began to have many, many complaints: His shirt was starched too stiff or it wasn't stiff enough. He wanted cornbread instead of biscuits. He wanted Mama to spend less money, but he didn't want "his young'uns going 'round, looking like orphans".

By some chance, we did not realize it Sunday through

Thursday, we were sure to hear by Friday and possibly all day long on Saturday just how hard he had to work for the few dollars that none of us seemed to appreciate.

As I grew older and gained more life experience, I earned a better insight. With it came a better understanding of Papa. He already had a heavy load to carry long before he lost his son or his mother and to a certain degree his brother, though he was very much alive.

Like most responsible men, he saw it as his obligation as a man to protect his family and make provisions that they may have the best life possible. Papa worked very hard to do just that, but when you are already being pressed hard between two boulders, the last thing you need to experience is an avalanche.

Papa had all of these pinned up emotions that he didn't know what to do with. Little Philip was his son too. Then his mother died. I can say without a doubt in my mind that he really loved them. But, he suppressed that pain. It seemed as if he denied himself the right to grieve. Sooner or later, he was bound to explode. And there were many.

Unfortunately, we had to bear the brunt of those explosions. The same family he felt so obliged to provide for and protect also became his unwilling, unintentional targets.

One of his favorite missiles was, "One of these days y'all gonna look up and I'll be gone on 'bout my business. What y'all gone do then?"

Another unfortunate truth is, Papa's leaving would not have alleviated our need for emotional bandages.

Each time Papa imposed that question, I would answer in my head, "Jump up and down for joy and then go over to Grandma's. Then I would remember that Grandma was gone and so was our safety net.

ESCAPE CLAUSE

When we are young, people tend to have many opinions about us:
More often than not, they label us as selfish, lazy, and ungrateful.
Some people call us, "brats".
They say, "We see ourselves as invincible.
And at times, we are oblivious to our surroundings."
However, these statements are not infinitive.

But, what if we like every other person in the human race are,
Sometimes vulnerable, sometimes hurting, sometimes fearful,
Sometimes lonely, sometimes sad, sometimes broken,
And sometimes enduring adult-sized battles?

When we are young and things appear to be unbearable,
We tend to run away, to hide, to go inside of ourselves,
Become angry and frustrated, oftentimes to the point of destruction.
Only later to be saddled with guilt and regret over choices we made in our haste to get away.

During our childhood stages, everything seems out of our hands.
Life happens to the young and the old, the rich and the poor,
It happens to the greatest and the lest,
Life's happenings aren't always easy for the mind to comprehend.

Right or wrong, no one consults us beforehand or afterwards.
We have to go with the flow, ride with the tide, and roll with the punches.
We get to share in the benefits as well as the deficits.
And we also have to reap the percussions.

And sometimes, when we have a lot of questions,
Life offers no suitable answers.
We, for a lack of a better alternative—run;
Later to learn that running was not the solution.

We seldom know the where, the what, or the when of it,
But we run anyhow though it's not always to a physical space.
When life and time and circumstance overwhelms us,
Plainly put, we too seek a way out.

Most times, we are gone long before we actually make our escape.
How could we have known?
Why didn't someone tell us?
Or would we have believed?
We ran straight out of the briar patch onto the back of a porcupine.

CHAPTER FOUR

Mama and Papa's fights became more frequent and more intense. Every time they got into it, she would run to their room hollering. Later, she would come out only to inflict her heartaches and headaches upon us.

Sometimes, I wondered if they would split up like my friend at school folks did. Sharon was miserable. She missed her Papa. And now, on top of everything else, they were moving away. At times, the whole family is made to suffer the consequences. To me, they always appeared to be the perfect family. If that could happen to them, what would become of us?

The thought of that always made me plead (in my head) for Papa to stay put. Though Mama and Papa had nearly become strangers to Alex and I, still, having Papa gone would've been a far worse nightmare than having him stay.

With Grandma next door, I felt we could get through almost anything. At least, I hoped we could. All of that changed when she grew sick and died. It seemed as quickly as an evening storm can arise on a hot, summer's day; death came in and snatched her away from us before I had any inkling of what was really happening.

Who was I going to turn to? Who would tell me, "Baby, don't you be fretting over nothing? Everything will be all right. You just wait and see." Although I didn't want to go with her, I wondered why she had left Alex and me alone in a world full of crazy.

Alex was little help. He was mischievous and silly.

We were trying to catch grasshoppers when the dog reappeared. We watched as it rested underneath the shade tree. He scratched himself, stood, stretched, then lifted up its' hind leg to pee. As I observed the dog, I thought about what Alex had said. I hit him on his arm. Hard!

"What did you do that for?" He asked. "Dummy, I almost had it!" He shouted, meaning the grasshopper.

"You know what you told me about Grandma! Well, did you see what that nasty, old dog just did? Grandma would've never done that in a million years." I assured him.

"She would if she was a dog. All dogs do that." He said.

"If Grandma was to come back, she would be an angel, maybe even a Princess or somebody like that, but she would never ever come back as an old, mangy dog. That's more like something you would come back as: Alex, the big, old, dumb dog that walks backwards, climbs trees like a cat, and moos like a cow." I teased.

Alex chased me. I giggled. We forgot about the grasshoppers as well as the morning's troubles. We were just children playing, living children's lives without having to worry about the whys or the hows of it all.

The dog joined in and started running behind us. At first, we thought it was chasing us. Its' tail waggled. The dog appeared to be laughing too. Then it rolled over several times. The dog wanted to play with us. It intended us no harm. I began to wonder again about what Alex had said.

The dog had shown up almost two weeks to the day after our Grandma was laid to rest in the graveyard behind the church. Afterwards, I couldn't even pass by the church without my eyes wondering in that direction.

Our baby brother, Philip Odell Wyatt was buried out there too. I still remember that cold day. It was not a regular funeral service like we had for Grandma with the church filled up with people hollering, lots of singing and with the Preacher preaching about what a good life she had lived.

Instead, we gathered in the graveyard. Reverend Bailey said a few words and then led us in prayer. Nobody sung a song for Little Philip. Nobody talked about his short life or how he laughed when you played with him or how he made a mess when he feed himself or how he used to lift up his arms for me to pick him up. Grandma used to say that I carried him around on my hip like an old woman. Alex nor I understood then that we would never see him or hear his laughter or clean up behind him ever again.

"Ashes to ashes and dust to dust" I heard Reverend Bailey say. Grandma took us back to the car. I saw Mama and Papa standing there, watching while they lowered that tiny white coffin with Little Philip in it down into that cold, dark, deep hole and then covered him up with dirt.

Mama was not the same after that sad day nor was Papa. It was as if someone came in, erased us off the canvas and immediately painted this sad little family in our place. They seemed caught up in one misery after another. Alex and I were tangled up in the debris and being dragged slowly along for the ride. Grandma wasn't there anymore so we had no choice except to go.

Every time I saw little boys and girls playing, it was hard not to think about Philip. When I saw Mamas doing motherly kinds of things or Papas holding onto their children's hands, I thought about us and the family we use to be. In those perfectly painted pictures, everyone always wore a smile. We were anything but perfect because in our picture, someone always appeared to be crying about something.

I DON'T WANT TO GO THERE ANYMORE

I don't want to go there anymore.
I don't want to ride back home without you.
Avoiding all of the spaces you used to fill with your love and laughter
helps me to pretend that you are still here just a little while longer.

I don't want to go there anymore.
The memories of you are like torture.
Sometimes, I can still feel your gentle touch and hear you speaking words of wisdom.
It always sends my heart racing to a place, a place where pain awaits me;
Only to leave me drowning myself in tears when I realize that you are gone;
Gone so far away from me.

I don't want to go there anymore.
It's so lonely without you.
Nothing seems the same and it will never be again.
I know that I must let go, but it's so hard to do.
Saying, "goodbye" seems like forever.

I don't want to go there anymore.
Your love was so genuine.
You listened to me even when I chattered on and on, endlessly.
You never called my dreams silly or too far out of reach.
Whenever I stumbled, you were there to catch me.
And when I fell, you lifted me up again.
You taught me that true love has no limits.
I don't want to go there anymore.

CHAPTER FIVE

Something else happened almost two weeks to the day after Grandma was dead and buried: Uncle Larry, his wife, Aunt Rita, and their four children moved into Grandma's house.

Papa was as hot as a blazing fire about it. I didn't understand why. Just because he and Uncle Larry weren't on speaking terms wasn't a good enough reason for Grandma's well-kept-up house to go to waste. If I could've, I would've taken Alex and moved in there myself.

While they were moving in, Papa was cursing up a blue streak. If his Mama, my Grandma could've heard him, she would've washed his old, dirty mouth out with lye soap. Mama just peeped out of the window, grunting and shaking her head, but I doubt if she really cared one way or the other. It's a wonder she didn't start hollering like she usually did every time Papa took a notion to pitch a fit. Mama cried so much, it's amazing she had any tears left.

Alex and I stayed out of the way. Whenever things went wrong (according to their thinking) both of us had learned that they wouldn't be in any mood to be patient with us.

All who knew Mama believed if ever given the choice, she would've sacrificed herself in order to save Philip. In my heart, I knew she would've done the same for Alex and me as well, but in my head, and with my eyes, I had become acquainted with a mama who found no pleasure in her living children anymore. She only grieved for the one who was dead. Little Philip was a happy child. He would've never wanted Mama to be what she had become: Trapped.

Blame and guilt on top of grief are some mighty heavy yokes to endure and/or overcome. It's possible for the strongest person to get crushed underneath the weight if we try to maneuver and shoulder the burden on our own. Yokes have a way of producing other yokes.

When we carry a weighty load, every now and then we have to make a shift. We can't afford to hang on and/or uphold a load that's breaking our backs. It's not necessary to present ourselves as some superhuman entity. If we don't find a way to put that thing down, it will put us down.

It appeared, tears had become Mama's only outlet; her only release. None of us saw her as a woman who couldn't cope with reality anymore crying out for help. In his own way, Papa was crying out for help too.

Papa wasn't always such a harsh man. He used to come home after a hard day at work and crawl around on the floor, giving "pony" rides to Little Philip. Whenever Alex climbed on, he would turn into a "bucking bronco", bucking and twisting and turning. Alex would hang on, until he got too tickled. During those times, Mama had a gleam in her eyes that let us know that we were her pride and joy.

I had outgrown "pony and bucking bronco rides", but sometimes, Papa brought home books for me. He called me, "Puddin'". He sneaked candy to us. Mama knew because Alex always went to her and opened up his mouth to show her what he had. We weren't perfect, but we were happy, and we were family.

After Philip, there were no more "pony or bucking bronco" rides; no more books or candy treats. I was no longer "his" Puddin'. We were no longer a family who shared a home. We just resided in a house.

And the way things were in our house: If Papa didn't like something, every one of us better act as if we didn't like it either. Mostly, Alex and I pretended except when it came to rutabagas. During those times, I believe they were one of the very few things that we agreed with Papa about. He didn't like them and neither did we. I suppose Mama just went along because she quit cooking them although she really liked them. I remember she always got herself a second helping while the rest of us pushed them around on our plates.

I guess Mama already knew what Alex and I had to learn eventually: It's much easier to go along with Papa than to oppose him. It just made for a more peaceful existence though it was a false sense of peace based upon Mama having to stifle her opinion in favor of his.

I have often wondered how Papa could've come from a woman as sweet as Grandma. She used to say that Papa was the spitting image of his Papa. I never knew him. I soon learned that Uncle Larry wasn't much different. To me, the way Papa and Uncle Larry acted was childish. At times, both of them went out of their way to be contrary. It became mighty hard to endure two spitting images.

BROTHERS

Brothers.
Yet, there something missing,
Something so vital,
A very necessary part of the equation.
It's fragile,
It exposes vulnerabilities,
It conquers fears,
It's something not easily detected by single-mindedness,
Nor viewed through the lens of natural, naked eyes.

Tempers flaring!
Name calling!
Finger pointing, placing blame!
Two been-grown men and their immature ways.

What could've caused this rift between them?
Was it something minute and then magnified?
Was it monumental, becoming bigger than the thing itself?
Was it constructed from crooked lies and misguided intentions?
Or woven out of preconceived notions and untimely,
unwelcomed truths?

THE PERFECTLY PAINTED PICTURE

Molded and mingled,
Folded and unfolded,
Intertwined and twice removed,
Individuals, units trying to live separate lives,
As if the other never existed.

Each seeking that something that causes oneness; cohesiveness,
Though it's sought out in ways that leaves the heart wondering:
Too silent!
Too vocal!
Too angry!
Too disgusted!
Like a card game gone bad,
Each man plays his hand,
But no one comes out the winner.
The hurt, the need, the words left unspoken,
Hidden underneath superficial things.

"Much too tired to take it."
"See no need in trying to make an effort."
"Things have gone too far, done stayed too long."
"No need in wasting strength on a hopeless situation."
They tell themselves and others,
Hoping excuses will help to justify their actions.

Lost in time!

Stuck in pride!

Not an inch or an ounce given,

The struggle has become the struggle,

Of which there is no rule or reason.

Yet, neither can bear to hear or speak the truth.

Hours turn into days,

Days become weeks,

Months roll by until they become years,

And then a decade.

Yes, time has passed and passed again and again,

But the stony place remains untouched, unbroken, and unchanged.

As from the beginning, they are brothers,

Bound together by flesh and blood and circumstance.

NOTHING CHANGES THAT!

Family! Kinsmen!

In spite of the erected walls determined to hold them captive.

Brothers!

CHAPTER SIX

One evening shortly after they had moved next door, in Grandma's house, Aunt Rita sent Marie, over to borrow a cup of sugar until Uncle Larry came in from work. Of course, Mama sent it. And surely, that was the right thing to do. Except, knowing Papa, I wish she could've found a better way and time to mention it to him. Mama just blurted it out at the supper table as if neighbors or family helping one another out was an unusual occurrence.

Papa's reaction was no surprise. He went on and on about how he couldn't afford to feed his family and another man's family too. He talked about how Uncle Larry was still a freeloading somebody, and how Uncle Larry had moved his family into their Mama's (Papa said, "his Mama's") house before she was good and cold. Papa told Mama, "The next time Larry can't keep in his house what his family needs, let them go without!"

There's a lot more to tell about that day and the many days that followed, but I want to mention this first: My Grandma was good and cold long before she was laid to rest. I know because I touched her. I held her hand for a few seconds. Grandma's hand was as hard as and felt as cold as a block of ice. It didn't feel anything like the hand I use to hold.

Death is hard. It's cold. It's still. It's silent. It's life—less. Yet, it's a part of the cycle.

Our house and Grandma's or Uncle Larry's house were so close, when one household was eating supper, the other household could practically taste it. So there was really no need for Papa to go over and tell Uncle Larry how he felt. I'm sure everyone in the house heard him the first time. Nonetheless, Papa stomped from the table before eating his usual six or seven biscuits, put his boots on and stormed out of the house.

I watched Mama out of the corner of my eye. She slid her chair back real easy, wiped her hands in her apron, eased over to the window like a cat that's about to pounce upon a mouse, and started peeping out.

Alex and I slipped out of the back door.

Uncle Larry and Cousin Leon were standing by the wood pile. Papa was standing at the edge of our yard. Until that day, it had been hard to tell where one yard begun and the other ended. Our yards never had nor ever needed any limits, but with Papa and Uncle Larry boundaries had become very necessary.

"Hey! Hey!" Papa hollered without bothering to address anyone in particular. "This here ain't no general store! If y'all need anything from now on, you best do your shopping there! We ain't got no sugar or nothing else over here to be lending out to you!"

Uncle Larry didn't say a word back to Papa. He did his talking to Leon who then ran into the house. I thought he might be going to get a shotgun or something, but he ran out empty-handed as far as I could see. He and Uncle Larry got into their car and took off down the road, real fast. That's one thing I could see he and Papa had in common.

Before long, Uncle Larry was knocking on our door. He handed Mama a whole bag of sugar. Mama said, "Thank you." Papa snatched the bag out of Mama's hand, poured some in a cup, and then took the rest back to the giver. "We don't need no hand-outs from that so and so!" He said just before he slammed the door behind him.

And so it went day after day. It seemed, during his every waking and at home hour, Papa found another reason to get upset with Uncle Larry. Uncle Larry started repaying him in kind.

There hadn't been any real peace around our house for quite a while. Now, it appeared, peace wasn't about to step its' feet into our yard much less inside our door. It may not have wanted any part of us, but I longed for it.

SPECULUM

The living became the dead,
Laughter turned into tears,
Family relationships shifted, producing adversaries.
Where peace once dwelled, turmoil had taken up residence.
And we who had no vote became enthralled in a life that did not reflect past times.

So like a lost child in the midst of a people whose language I could not understand,
I moved desperately throughout the crowd in need of someone to relate to,
someone to acknowledge my existence, my pain
but neither they nor I was able to comprehend.

Journeying from one place to another, looking into the faces of strangers,
seeking the familiar, but there was no recognition, no communication, no connection.
Then, it occurred to me—I must be invisible.

I, in search of validation, noticed a people, who had eyes without vision,
ears, but no one was listening, a voice, yet no one was speaking,
light and strength and joy, but choosing neither.

Instead, living life in a speculum; a mirrored image of their circumstances;
a limited imitation; an optical illusion; a counterfeit reflection of their former selves.
No. It was not I who had changed, but them.

CHAPTER SEVEN

Whatever happened between Papa and Uncle Larry must've been pretty bad. Although I was just a child, it seemed to me, they could've worked it out if they'd really wanted to; if not for themselves, for their wives and children.

Old, dumb Alex got on my nerves mighty bad sometimes. Sometimes, I hit him or acted mean to him. He did the same to me too, but in the end, he was/is still my brother. After Grandma died, he was the only one who understood the mess we had to live through day after day. Common sense told me that I needed Alex and he needed me. I prayed that Papa and Uncle Larry would reach that same understanding before it was too late.

Even walking home from the bus stop had gotten to be a reason for sadness though it was also sort of comical. Alex and I walked on one side of the road. Our cousins walked on the other side. While waiting on the bus, we didn't say a single word to one another. I would've if they would've, which sadly, oftentimes, is the story of our lives. They hadn't done one thing to Alex or me that I knew of. Neither had we done anything to them. The trouble was between our Papas.

Whenever Alex and I talked, I could tell that they were listening. We listened whenever they talked amongst themselves. Sometimes, I wanted to laugh, but I didn't dare. Cousin Leon was real silly. He was dumb too; just like his Cousin Alex. I reckoned all boys were born with something that made them act the way they did, but I could see that Cousins Marie, Vanessa, and Trina knew how to get him back.

THE PERFECTLY PAINTED PICTURE

One day in particular, I got sort of mad with them. We were walking home from the bus stop as usual: them on one side, us on the other. It (that's what Alex and I named the dog) ran up to us wagging his tail and barking.

First, It jumped up on Alex as if he wanted to play or had been waiting all day to see him. Then he ran over to our cousins just like he knew them. Marie took a piece of sandwich out of her sack and feed it to him. Leon rubbed It's back and said, "You sure are a nice dog."

Alex couldn't take anymore. I couldn't either, but I didn't say anything. "Come here, It. Come on." Alex tried to whistle as he hit the side of his leg.

It ran back and forth, running from us to our cousins. He even ran in circles as if he was trying to put on a show for us. Although I knew that It was not my Grandma in any way, shape, form, or fashion, I later thought about how he'd acted. I knew if she'd been there, she would've done the same thing. Grandma would see all of us as her grandchildren. She would've treated us equally, and would've never made a difference between any of us.

I soon got over my resentment. I told myself that I didn't care if It played with them or not. He really wasn't our dog anyway. I didn't want to become like Papa and make It go along with something that he didn't agree with or like doing or something that caused other people to hurt.

Things were going fine and dandy between our cousins, It, and Alex and I. We had come to an unspoken agreement: My cousins, It and us, every morning seemed to have been the perfectly painted picture. Things continued that way until Papa and Uncle Larry got hold of the picture, and started smearing the paint and poking holes into the paper.

Papa, who had told Alex and me as plain as daylight, "Don't be feeding that mutt so he can go on 'bout his business", suddenly appeared to have a change of heart. He had said, "I've already got enough mouths to feed. I ain't looking to take on no more."

Some people tend to change their minds only when it suits their purposes. As soon as he saw Uncle Larry's children, who are also his very own flesh and blood nieces and nephew playing with It, he laid claim to him. It then became, "his" young'uns dog.

Papa grabbed It up and carried him to our back yard. He wasn't bothered in the lest that It growled when he did it. I thought he was going to bite Papa for sure, but too bad for It if he had.

Alex said. "Grandma is showing her displeasure to Papa for how he's acting."

I hit Alex. He hit me back. Our cousins stood in their yard, looking real puzzled. Papa seemed to care less about how any of us felt, including It. I could tell that he wanted to come and play some more. I wished that he could've too. He was having fun, but now, Papa had him tied to the back fence. Its' freedom had been taken away just like that; without a second thought. I knew how he felt. Alex knew. And perhaps, our cousins knew too.

The very next evening, I was at the clothesline, taking in the wash when Uncle Larry drove up. He took a box out of the back of the car. Then he reached inside the box, took out what resembled a very large ball of brown fuzz, and sat it on the ground. It was a puppy! He had brought a dog home!

Uncle Larry knocked on the back door. My cousins came outside. They saw the puppy. They started laughing, and jumping around, and playing with the puppy. I could hear them thanking their Papa for the dog. They were happy, real happy as if they were in a perfectly painted picture.

I couldn't help being real happy along with them even though their happiness had nothing to do with me directly, but it did indirectly. That is, until my mind got to thinking. Knowing Papa the way I do, and seeing that Uncle Larry is practically his spitting image, I wondered if Uncle Larry had brought the dog home because he knew that it would make his children happy? Or did he do it just to spite Papa? Either way, they had themselves a dog.

And either way, I didn't see peace coming any closer. Thankfully, oftentimes, we look for the answers to our questions or the solutions to our problems to come through one door, but they enter through another. They may not come according to our expectations or in what we consider to be a timely manner, or even to our liking or understanding, but if we trust God, wait on Him to direct us, it will come.

As I matured, my faith along with time and experience has taught me: If I don't become fainthearted during the process, some fruit or a reward or a change will be manifest.

LIFE GOES ON

Life goes on.
In spite of how things appear in our little corner of the world,
Whether we're in a season of jubilee or grief,
The Earth continues to spin on its' axis.
There are still sunrises and sunsets,
Nature does not relax or take a rest,
Summer, Winter, Spring, and/or Fall does not cease.
The transformation of caterpillars into butterflies remains unbroken.
The beauty of the rosebud is still able to draw the attention away from the thorn.
The eagle continues to soar in the open skies.
Fish still need water to survive.
And life goes on.

CHAPTER EIGHT

In the Spring when the Easter lilies were in bloom, Mama's tulips that she didn't bother with anymore were coming up in spite of it all, and our lives that I believed couldn't get any worse, turned into an eyes-wide-open nightmare.

After school, Alex and I came in through the back door as usual. Somehow, we knew that we didn't have any company. We seldom did. Yet, we could hear Mama talking out loud as if she was holding a conversation with someone else. We followed her voice up to the living room. She was sitting in the middle of the floor, going through a box of Little Philip's things. She kept crying out for him as though he was in the room with her.

"What is it, Mama?" I asked.

"What did y'all do with my Philip? Where's my baby?" She hollered in a voice that was different, and seemed to hit every nerve in my body although I had almost grown use to her hollering.

Alex backed up against the wall. His eyes were as wide as two fifty cent coins. I was scared too, but I kept trying to talk to Mama. She got up off the floor and started knocking things over, still calling out for Philip. She was making a pure mess. Nothing I did or said made a bit of difference to her, and nothing she did or said made any sense to me.

I knew one thing for sure: Even if she tore our house to pieces looking, she wasn't about to find Little Philip. He was in the graveyard, lying next to Grandma. For a brief moment, I forgot all about Grandma being gone too. I did what had always come as natural to me as breathing whenever trouble came: I ran over to Grandma's. Alex was on my heels. I knocked on the door as if I was being chased by that fire-breathing dragon I sometimes envisioned.

"What is it child?" Aunt Rita asked, after she'd opened the door.

I opened my mouth, but nothing could or would come out.

"I said, 'what is it?' What in the world done got into you?" She asked, taking me by the shoulders.

"It's Mama! She ain't acting right!" I managed to say.

"And she's over there, tearing our house to pieces, looking for our little brother, but he ain't with us no more!" Alex broke in.

"Oh, my Lord!" was all Aunt Rita said before running down the steps, hurriedly making her way over to our house.

When she opened the door, things were even worse than they had been just a few minutes before.

"Lillie Mae, this is Rita. What's the matter, honey? You got to get a hold of yourself. Do you need to lie down?" Aunt Rita asked in a voice that I suspected was meant to soothe Mama, but didn't. Things only got worse.

Mama turned on Aunt Rita. "What did you do with my baby? I know you got him! He belongs to me! I'm his Mama! He belongs to me!" She cried.

Aunt Rita went into the kitchen, and started dialing numbers on the telephone. I heard her saying, "We need you to send somebody to Apple Orchard Road. That's Route 4 Box 219. What's the matter? I don't know what the matter is. All I know is, there's a woman in here tearing her house down, looking for her dead young'un whose been in the ground for better than two years now. Beyond that, I can't tell you nothing. Yes. We'll be looking out for you."

She then called the operator to get the number for Papa's job. After waiting for some time, she began speaking. "This is Rita. I don't have time for that foolishness man. I'm calling about your wife. It appears she done went out of her head. You better be getting home as fast as you can."

Papa and the Rescue Squad must've been in a race because they arrived around the same time. I believe Papa came into the house ready to start up something. When he saw Mama and the mess our house was in, he couldn't say a word; not one single word. He opened up his mouth, but nothing would come out. In my whole life, I'd never seen him speechless. Except Papa was more than speechless, he looked as if he had seen a ghost.

When the people put Mama into the Rescue vehicle, she was still calling out for Little Philip. They stuck her in the arm with a needle. I felt bad for her because I hate needles. At the same time, I hoped that it would help Mama.

CRISIS

Along with the unanswerable, all of the whys, and what ifs,
questions that plagued her during most of her days and all of her nights,
came the heaviness, until it slowly and deliberately wore her down like
burdensome weights on an already yoked back.

To add insult to injury as if the loneliness and despair that accompanied
her empty arms and broken heart were not enough,
disappointment, guilt, angrier, and fear were also determined to have their say.
They sprang up in her field of sorrows as if they were a crop to be harvested
and appreciated for its plenty.

It seemed, the husband who had vowed to be with her for the better,
and for the worse had mentally abandoned her at the worst possible times imaginable.
The children, the children she dearly loved were now a constant reminder of her loss.
And the mother-in-law who became a mother to her had died, taking all of her love,
prayers, and wisdom with her to the grave.

There was no plan involved, no expected or accepted escape clause.
"Unbearable", a song without lyrics,
"Hopeless", the music was without rhythm,
Nevertheless, played over and over again in her mind, coercing her to dance,
dance into its opened door, into a place unknown.
So dance she did.

CHAPTER NINE

As Papa walked out of the door, Aunt Rita said, "Pete, don't you be worrying about the young'uns. I'll take them over to the house and give them their supper. When Larry gets home, I'll come over and clean up some of this."

Papa didn't say a word. He just raised his hat and scratched his head. I waited for him to at least say, "thank you" or something, but he never did. I supposed, since Aunt Rita had to live with Uncle Larry, Papa's spitting image every day, maybe she didn't really expect it, but I did.

It really was mighty nice of her to offer. I don't believe too many people would've, especially after seeing the mess our house was in. Perhaps, some people would've been hard-pressed to show much empathy solely due to Papa's most of the time peculiar acting ways.

When we got over to Aunt Rita's, Alex and I didn't quite know what to do with ourselves. I kept thinking about Mama. I couldn't help hoping that Papa wouldn't get to wherever they were taking her and start acting like his same old self.

By the time Uncle Larry came in, my stomach felt like it had joined up with my backbone as Grandma used to say. In other words, I was hungry. Aunt Rita had prepared a meal for six. She had eight for supper. I hoped she had cooked enough. I didn't want them to go lacking because of us.

She had cooked more than a plenty. The biscuits were piled high on a platter setting in the middle of the table. There was also a smaller platter with fried ham slices, a large bowl of great northern beans, and another bowl of stewed apples. Everything was real good. I hunched Alex hard after he'd asked for seconds although I could've eaten seconds too, maybe even thirds.

THE PERFECTLY PAINTED PICTURE

Aunt Rita can cook almost as good as Grandma could. Still, I didn't want it said that Alex and I came over there, and tried to eat them out of house and home.

I was mighty tempted when Aunt Rita said, "Baby, y'all can have some more if you want it. Eat 'til you get full. Y'all are welcome to it. If this ain't enough, I'll fix you something else." I also saw Uncle Larry's expression when she said that too.

"No thank you, Aunt Rita. Alex and I are full. Thank you for the supper." I said.

"Yes ma'am, Aunt Rita, I'll take another biscuit please. Can I have one to take home too?" Alex asked.

I pinched him on his leg. He knew better than that. Where in the world had his home training went? He better be glad Papa didn't hear him begging. Alex only looked at me as if to ask, "Dummy, what you do that for?" He knew. And I knew that he knew.

CHAPTER TEN

Papa came home late. I was still sitting up, but I sure was ready to lie down in my bed. Uncle Larry had told us that we might as well stretch out and get some shut eye. He sounded just like Papa. I kept waiting.

Aunt Rita had put a plate up for Papa. She gave it to him when he came for us. He grunted, but again, I didn't hear the words, "thank you" or anything else leave his mouth. Aunt Rita just smiled. Then she asked about Mama. Papa's bad manners seemed to be the least of her concerns.

Papa said. "She's doing all right. They want to keep an eye on her for a day or two. When I left, she was sleeping like a baby."

Surely, Mama had come a long way if she was doing as well as Papa had said. I hoped with every hope that could fit into my child-sized body that he was telling the truth. At least, she got a chance to escape from some of her troubles which was more than the rest of us could do. Not that I wanted to go so far as having to go out of my mind to get away from them; not even for a little while.

I waited for Papa. I thought about Mama. She probably could get better more quickly if she had something else to think on besides a dead baby, an ungrateful man, Alex and me who she considered bad enough to be labeled, "the devil's chirren for sure", and family next door who didn't act or get treated like family.

Right then and there, I made up my mind that I would do better. I would tell Alex that he had to do better too, for Mama's sake, for the sakes of all of us. Papa was another story. Nobody could tell him much of anything. Usually, Papa did as Papa pleased whether we liked it or not.

Since Grandma, Aunt Rita was the first adult I believed I could invite into that special place in my heart, a place I thought I had locked away forever. She was easy to love.

I was caught up in my own thinking so I didn't hear all that Papa had said about Mama, but I heard Aunt Rita say, "That's mighty good to hear." Her facial expressions were saying something totally different, something I didn't understand.

"Well, I reckon, we best be getting back to the house. Goodnight to y'all." Papa said.

Alex wiped his eyes and staggered toward the door. I stood up and headed that way too, but something stopped me in my tracks, turned me toward Aunt Rita, it then wrapped my arms around her. "Thank you, Aunt Rita for being so nice to us. Thank you for helping us with Mama. And thank you for what you did at the house." I heard myself saying.

"Baby, I couldn't have done any less. We're family: for the better and for the worse. Now, y'all better go on and get yourselves to bed before the sandman comes in and catches you wide awake." She said, smiling.

Alex ran over to the table to get the biscuits Aunt Rita had wrapped up for him, the ones his old, greedy posterior had begged for. He might've been sleepy, but he wasn't ever too sleepy to forget about something to eat.

Uncle Larry sat in the chair, watching, or pretending to watch a show on the television. He didn't speak a word to Papa and neither did Papa address him. I should've known: If their very own, sweet Mama dying couldn't help them to mend fences, bury the hatchet, or do whatever it was going to take to make them act like brothers again, certainly, my Mama going out of her head, being taken away in a Rescue Wagon to Lord only knows where, wasn't going to be enough either.

But like Grandma used to say, "Honey, you can still hope even when it appears you don't have nothing else."

I prayed that I still had plenty of hope left over. I had already used a lot of it up on things that hadn't changed, and didn't look as if they were ever going to. Our perfectly painted picture had become a perfectly painted mess. It was going to take a miracle to make things better.

HAND AND HEART

You offered me your hand.

I took hold of it.

I was uncertain;

In fact, quite apprehensive though I tried to hide it.

My need of you was disconcerting.

Your kindness seemed to challenge something within me.

You tried to assure me that there was no harm intended.

Your hand was there to lift me;

There only to help.

Without reason, I silently resisted.

Yet, I knew, I needed you.

So with stubborn pride pushed aside,

I took hold and held on tightly.

Later, I learned that your hand was an extension of your heart.

And I just want to say, "Thank you".

CHAPTER ELEVEN

Whether Papa liked it much or appreciated it any, Aunt Rita continued to watch out for Alex and me. She even left a supper plate for Papa. In the mornings, he usually tried to put something together for breakfast. The truth is: Papa couldn't cook a lick.

Grandma had taught me how to make oatmeal. It was the only thing that I knew how to cook. With a little sugar, cinnamon, butter and milk mixed in, it tasted all right; nothing to brag on though. Nevertheless, it was by far tastier than Papa's hard, dried, scrambled eggs, burned side meat, and lumpy grits. We could see that he was having a real hard time eating his own cooking. We thanked God for It, who seemed to appreciate whatever we feed to him.

Our cousins' dog, Walnut (named mostly for the color of her mane) grew into a real fine dog. It wasn't doing too badly. Pretty was a lot to ask for where he was concerned. Still, he was beautiful to us because we loved him. The dogs became good friends. Our cousins, Alex, and I did too. However, Papa and Uncle Larry were another story.

Mama remained absent both physically and emotionally for months. Her stay in the hospital lasted much longer than the few days that Papa had first mentioned. I missed her in a different sort of way. Alex missed her. In his own way, Papa missed her too.

Since Little Philip's death, so many days had come and gone when Mama was right in the house with us, but at the same time, not really with us. Thinking on it now, no matter where she was or who she was with, she always seemed to be somewhere off in a distant place filled with loneliness and misery. The death of our baby brother left a gaping hole in her heart. Overtime, it seemed to grow deeper and wider.

****

Aunt Rita appeared to be a bright, shining star in the midst of a midnight sky. It was like standing, looking out of a window, your face pressed against the glass pane, and anxiously trying to wish the rainy day away, but the clouds refuse to budge. Then seemingly out of the blue, the rain cease, the sun breaks through, and a beautiful rainbow stretches itself across the sky.

Nonetheless, I told myself that I wasn't going to allow myself to get too attached to her. I was really close to Grandma and Little Philip, and they had been taken away quicker than a snowflake left out in the hot sun. I wanted to feel close to Mama and Papa again, but they no longer took delight in the living. Their time was spent grieving for the dead. Thankfully, I still had Alex, and he still had me.

I believe it would've been almost unbearable if another loved one had been snatched away from me. I had witnessed up close what heartache could do if and when we allowed it to come in and set up housekeeping. I certainly didn't want to hurt so bad until I became like Mama who had been broken into bits and pieces by her heartache. So I decided that it was best if I kept my distance. From a child's prospective, it was evident, bad things happened to people when you get too close to them.

I often wondered about life and how things sometimes/oftentimes turned out opposite from what seemed most sensible: Little Philip's death was terribly painful, and hard to understand, but it should've brought our family closer together, but it didn't.

Then it seemed, before the dust could settle, our Grandma died. We were left with tragedy upon tragedy.

When Uncle Larry moved his family next door, in the beginning, it felt like a series of ill winds had blown in, and targeted our family to reap havoc upon.

With every passing day, we became more unglued, unscrewed, and unhinged. Whatever had been holding us together in the past had given way under the pressure of many shed tears, heartache, and people expecting other people to fix, and make things right that they had no power to change.

Life became a daily and most often unnecessary struggle: People fighting for the sake of fighting, but mostly out of stubbornness and false pride. People unwilling to yield because being right became more important than being brothers. While at the same time, other people refused to fight, and instead yielded to the heartache, and allowed grief to become their pillow until it made them broken and bitter.

Mama and Papa stopped attending church altogether after Grandma's funeral service. They'd attended only three or four times after Little Philip's burial. Afterwards, Mama would be so pitiful, and Papa would be so angry. They acted as if they blamed God for their troubles. Alex and I had practically grown up in church. Now, we were like driftwood.

One Saturday evening, I shined my black patent leather shoes with petroleum jelly until they shined like new money. I told Alex to shine his shoes, and get his church clothes ready. We were going to Sunday service. I was on a mission. In Sunday school class, we had been taught that God is everywhere. I believed He was at church, but I didn't see Him at our house anymore. I needed to go to church and ask Him if He would please come back to our house. We really needed Him.

YOU WERE THERE

Oh Lord, You saw,

You knew,

And You cared.

You heard my cry.

You were there.

So many nights, I lay in bed,

Wide awake, shedding tears,

Tears seasoned with salt as well as pain.

I cried over our past that seemed a whole lifetime gone,

Because of our present,

And for a future I could not envision.

In the darkness, in the still of the night, my pillow wet with tears,

I prayed and prayed, "Oh Lord, please come and see about us.

I knew You were there.

I could hear the crickets chirping.

I could see the bright stars twinkling as though they were
dancing across the sky,
Along with the moonlight that abated the darkness,
And I could smell the sweet fragrance of the honeysuckle
blooms being
ushered in by the gentle breezes blowing through
my opened window.

Oh Lord, You saw,
You knew,
And You answered.
You were so close, I felt, I could reach out and touch You.
I whispered Your name over and over again until it began
to fill me up.
Oh Lord, I knew you were there!

CHAPTER TWELVE

It was Summer time before another bad thing happened; not that all of the other bad things had been resolved. Although there had been no whirlwind of good blowing our way, and peace seemed like a dream whose time had long passed, for a while, life gave us exactly what we expected: the mundane, a just putting one foot in front of the other existence. Considering everything our family had been through, and continued to go through, I guess, the ordinary should've been viewed as a blessing.

Grandma had taught me that God is The Only One we can really count on. She said, "Baby, He won't change a lick. Whether we're walking on rose petals, egg shells, or pins and needles, He is still God. He is the same: yesterday, today, and forever. Everything and everyone else is subject to change faster than a salamander can switch colors.

I learned that I should always trust and depend on God. Grandma would say, "When trouble comes, and it will, and it seems like it's coming at you from every side, look up to The One who can see you through. Honey, He will come to see about you.

"One of these days, my time on this earth will be over, and as much as I love you, I won't be here for you to run to no more, but my Jesus is a Hiding Place. He is a Solid Rock, and a True Friend. He's The One you can call on in the midnight hour. He's never too busy. He never sleeps or slumbers. And He's never too late.

"The Lord has brought me through storms, heartaches, disappointments, sickness, grief—so much. I done had to stare the valley in the face a whole heap more than I ever celebrated being on the mountaintop. And child, even with all of that, I know that life ain't through with me yet.

"Sometimes, I had to come in on broken pieces, but I made it, in spite of the splinters. Though I've been tested, I've been tried, and Lord knows I've had some tribulations, but I kept on believing. I kept right on praying and thanking my God. Baby Girl, you hear me and hear me well: There's always another side. The test has another side so does the trial and the tribulation. Old slew-foot may want you to believe that things gone always be this way, but it ain't so. Always believe in the report of the Lord.

"You gone come out of this thing, and you're coming out strong; you and Alex. It may not look or feel like it now, but you can't go off of how things look or feel. They'll deceive you. I don't know when, and I don't know how, and I may not be here to see it. Nevertheless, I believe."

Through my Grandma's love for and faith in God, her wisdom,

along with time, experience and understanding, I received some very valuable lessons on life, hope, love and change. I continue to apply and hold onto that teaching as well as pass them on. They are a vital and very necessary part of my heritage. Over the years, and through my own faith, I've sought and found solace, peace, and strength in them.

We were outside playing: our cousins, Alex and me, It and Walnut. Everything was going fine and dandy. Mr. Oscar the Egg Man had stopped by to make deliveries at our house and Uncle Larry's. First, he talked with Papa, but mostly to bring eggs and to settle up his bill. Then he walked across the yard to do the same thing all over again, except, he and Uncle Larry really talked. They were laughing and carrying on just like the men do outside, on the church grounds after Sunday service.

When the Egg Man started backing up, It got away from us, and ran out toward the truck, barking. Before we could make a step or call him or anything, It was hollering. Mr. Oscar stopped his truck. Papa came out front and so did Uncle Larry.

Poor It had his leg raised. When the Egg Man touched him, he growled. We stood around in a daze. At that time, all I could think about was how trouble doesn't even leave the dogs alone. Trouble will and does jump on everybody and everything it can jump on.

"I'm so sorry, chirren. I didn't see him! I'm so sorry!" Mr. Oscar kept saying. He was really shook up.

"We'll take care of him." Uncle Larry tried to assure him. Papa tapped him on the shoulders a few times.

So It was a him. We weren't really sure nor had we bothered to ask. I knew then, not that I had believed my brother, Alex before: The dog couldn't be our Grandma, especially, not coming back as a boy.

Papa and Uncle Larry carried It up on our front porch. Our cousins, Alex and I gathered around, looking to see what they were going to do to him. Walnut looked on too.

"Leon, Marie, go to the house and ask your Mama to send us a rag out here. Son, put some water in that old foot tub I keep 'round back." Uncle Larry called out.

They, Papa and Uncle Larry, cleaned up Its' wounds and bandaged his leg. Afterwards, they sat him back down on the ground. It was limping. Walnut went over and started sniffing on him. In a dog's kind of way, maybe Walnut was telling It how sorry she was that he had gotten hurt.

"Y'all take it easy with him now. He won't be able to keep up with y'all for a while." Papa said.

"Those young'uns of ours sure do love those dogs, don't they?" I heard Uncle Larry say to Papa.

"I'm just glad that things won't no worse than they were. My young'uns done already been through enough." I heard Papa answer back.

My heart flooded with glad. Something had finally come along to melt the ice around their cold, angry hearts. In a round-about way, It had done it.

I thought about Grandma, but not for the same reasons as before. I knew, no matter what anyone said, including dumb, old Alex: It was not and had never been our Grandma in any way, shape, form or fashion. I thought about her up in heaven, looking over her children, smiling, and telling God, "thank You."

LOVE AND FORGIVENESS

Oftentimes, we sit and wait, waiting for the other one to reach out,
to make the first move, to offer the first apology, to concede;
All the while, treating each other like arch enemies.

Acting as if it doesn't matter that we carry the same last name,
were birthed through the very same womb, and nursed from the same breast.
At times, ate from the same spoon, and drank from the same cup.

Do you remember how Mama used to pull those heavy quilts over us at night?
And how we use to laugh and giggle because we thought that we had gotten
away with some boyish prank?

It's funny now, but we were always surprised when she caught us in our mess.
Somehow, she always knew.
Mama would catch and reel us in just like the fish we use to catch down at Silver Lake.

Remember the time you fell in?
We went home muddy.

THE PERFECTLY PAINTED PICTURE

My heart sank at the thought of something bad happening to you.
And that's why I jumped in.

We were scared, but we still had those three little fish tied on a string.
One look at us and Mama knew.
After a warm bath, some clean clothes, and a hot meal, off to bed we went.
That night, we overheard Mama praying, "Thank You Lord for watching over my boys".
We thought that we had a good one coming for sure,
but she never uttered another word about it.

After Papa died, you and I were all the family she had left.
She loved us, man.
We were her pride and joy.

Over the years, we caused her to shed many tears.
We are brothers.
Yet, we were at war.
It's been so long, neither of us can remember why.
I guess the discomfort of it became our comfort.

Here we are so big and strong, older and somewhat wiser,
finally realizing how fragile are the emotions,
how stubborn a will left to its' own unyielding self,
left to its' own devices.

Reluctant to bend, refusing to break,
too afraid to appear weak when quite the opposite is true.
So much time has come and gone, but it's not too late
for us to act like we're brothers again.

Apologies given and accepted, long overdue,
much like the embrace they shared,
an embrace that began as a simple stranger to stranger handshake,
ended with a cough meant to disguise, a tear quickly stroked away,
inhale,
exhale.

Then, in unison, as with the same mind, and in the same breath,
they said, "Man, I'll give almost anything for Mama to see us now".
And they both knew without another word being spoken,
Love and forgiveness.

CHAPTER THIRTEEN

Mama finally came home. On some days, her eyes looked cloudy, and empty as if she'd somehow vacated the premises. On the most difficult days, it was as if she'd been hidden behind a heavy curtain that want, need, and motherhood weren't allowed to penetrate, and even love's effort became laborious as it tried to saturate the divide. I imagined us being involved in a game of 'hide and seek', but no one knew the rules; not even Mama. At times, she was extremely quiet. Overall, she smiled more, cried less, and she didn't call Alex and me, "the devil's chirren for sure" anymore. Surely, we were mighty glad about that.

Papa changed too. Maybe having to do some of the cleaning, cooking, washing, and ironing did him a world of good. He stopped complaining about everything like he used to do. Things seemed to suit him better. Apparently, he realized the difference between the significant and the immaterial. He had a lot to bear, but Alex and I helped out. Uncle Larry and Aunt Rita helped as much as possible.

Papa touched Mama more. However, he also sometimes treated her as though she might break. Perhaps, the possibility of that happening again was always in the back of his mind. For the most part, the process was painstakingly slow, but he began to be more openly affectionate toward her. It's a shame that things had to go so far and stay so long before Alex and I saw our parents really embrace one another again. So much wasted time. Life's ruler doesn't always measure in straight lines, or by yards, feet and inches. Nor does life always chronicle time by hours, minutes and seconds.

Our crying may last for a season, but if we hold on, we shall also have a season of delight.

A shifting had definitely taken place within our family. It was manifested by both visible and invisible things: Whenever Papa talked to us, it wasn't just to bark out more orders. He acted as if he really did like us again; even loved us. And moreover, he was glad to have his family around; all of us.

I didn't hit on Alex as much as I use to, but I would still let him have it every now and then. Our cousins: Marie, Trina, and Vanessa became my best friends. We read books, took walks, talked about things, particularly, how dumb boys were. However, over time, our tune changed. We laughed a lot too. It certainly felt good to laugh more than I cried.

Life happens. At some point, we have or will encounter trouble. Separations, divorce, disappointments, financial stresses, illness, employment issues, addictions, misplaced trust, betrayal, loneliness, fears, death, and etc. can leave us in a state of barely hanging on, just surviving. The struggle itself can put a strangle hold on us, causing us to be too afraid to hold on and too afraid to let go. Howbeit, the struggle can be no bigger than our perception of it. Oftentimes, it's how we view it that will determine how and/or if we get through it.

Those things that rise up to oppose us, we view as giants more often than not. In our eyes, we're faced with an insurmountable situation, and according to our perception, our chances of prevailing are nil to none. However, I've learned that every struggle doesn't come to destroy. Though the enemy will try to bait us, tell us that the fight is over, and we're down for the count. He is a liar! We can't just lie down and die, but we can speak death over that thing that tries to torment us. For every Goliath, there is a David. We don't have to fight alone. When we put our trust in God, the conflict is not ours anyway. He will never abandon us nor will we be made ashamed for putting our trust in Him. God never promised us that the enemy or floods wouldn't come. He promised us that He would lift up a standard against him. In times of trouble, trial, and temptation, He will provide us with a way of escape.

People, even those closest to us may try to remind us of who we are (in their minds), where we came from, what we lack, and how incapable we are of defeating and/or overcoming the situation. If David had listened to his oldest brother, he would've went back home. If he'd listened to Saul, he would've been weighted down. Instead, he listened to God, Who equipped him for battle with a slingshot and five smooth stones, but it took only one. Faith overrides perception.

Goliath reminds me of a one-man demolition squad or a public nuisance. His confidence was in himself, the Philistine army, and their god. He didn't start his bullying and boasting on the day that David showed up. He had been a tormentor for quite some time: morning and evening for forty days. Sadly, his tactics were working. He was able to supplant fear into the hearts and the minds of King Saul and the Israelite army.

Unfortunately, many of the distresses we face didn't begin with us. Some things have been around for a long time; maybe even for generations.

Everyone isn't comfortable with open dialogue. Family members may "sweep" issues under the rug rather than discuss them. They may deny the existence thereof. They may use other tactics to keep it out of the forefront; like whitewashing. Some members will not approach a subject if a hostile environment is created around it. If Aunt or Uncle "Not So" gets belligerent at the very mention of certain things, other members will try to avoid it, for the sake of keeping the peace.

Nevertheless, the thing is in full view. It permeates every

birthday celebration, family reunion, wedding ceremony, funeral service, and any other occasion for family gatherings. Trying to cut through some of our family issues is like attempting to cultivate the soil with cooking utensils; tedious, but not impossible.

Countless families have been crushed under the weight of the proverbial elephant. While it may be disguised as something else, it's an elephant just the same. Putting a lampshade on its' head doesn't make it a lamp. Pretending takes concerted, concentrated effort.

Over the years, I've learned several things about family relationships by experience and through observation: When we set out to evade an issue, it oftentimes becomes invasive, and can eventually become pervasive. In other words, avoiding and/or suppressing issues, especially within ourselves will not cause them to abate. They can become more aggressive instead, and quite possibly take on a nature of their own, having the puissance (power) to effluence (flow or issue).

Mama and Papa's issues chose to deal with them. Perhaps, sharing their concerns with one another could've lessened their affect. Both exhibited behaviors that most likely stemmed from the pain they felt. Suppressed? Not hardly. Mama's crying spells, her eventual breakdown; Papa's angrier, his withdrawal emanated from open, festered wounds that were denied an opportunity to start the healing process. They were also denied a voice.

Grandma's name was seldom referenced. I didn't hear Mama utter Little Philip's name once after he was buried. That is, not until the day she went away. She and Papa's emotions were like dammed up waters. Sooner or later, they were going to burst. Whether they discussed it or not, everyone was affected by the changes and the losses within our family structure, including Alex and I.

Life plays by its own rules. Time and chance happens to us all.

Does that mean that we don't have an option?

No!

Or that our only alternative is to go with the flow?

Absolutely not!

Or that we should succumb to the pressure?

Never!

A WORD PLAY ON LIFE

Our experiences in life can and do affect us in several different ways.
One person's hardship is another's challenge, but pain for someone else.
Different cause, different effect;
Different outlook, different outcome:

The <u>effluence</u> of the residuals that stem from our personal trials, tests, tribulations, or triumphs
Will influence us in some way; either adversely or favorably.
They may also sway us to become apathetic or responsive.

Our struggles, conditions, circumstances and situations
Can, if we let them, make us unpliable;
Have us spinning in a downward spiral, out of control;

Our insecurities, regrets, bitterness, intolerances, and fears fermenting until we become <u>effluvial</u>;
And leave us emanating an invisible, toxic stench
At the point of our flow, that which strains and drains us.
Or they can lead us into our destiny, our purpose; the very reason we are here.

But wouldn't it be great to endure life's oppositions, and still come out smelling like roses?

To become <u>efflorescent</u>: flourishing, blossoming, maturing, and producing good fruit, in spite of.

What if, out of our heartache and brokenness, we could emerge <u>effulgent</u>?
What if we became beacons of light, love, and hope?
What if the end result of our issues made us better?
More appreciative,
More thoughtful,
More caring,

And as we surrender our all to God,
Allowing Him to realign and reign in our lives,
He Who can heal our wounds, and turn our battle scars into badges of honor.

Thereafter, we become <u>efficacious</u>,
Instead of self-confident and self-willed,
We are empowered to sufficiently fulfill and accomplish our intended purpose;
And all that we were equipped and designed for.

CHAPTER FOURTEEN

Walnut and It became mama and papa to seven puppies. One looked like It. Three looked like Walnut. The others just looked like themselves. Papa and Uncle Larry told us that we couldn't keep all of them. Our cousins picked out the brown one with the tiny white spot on his head. Alex and I picked out the one that looked just like It. The others were taken in too. Mr. Oscar, the Egg Man, came and picked out the one he called, "the runt of the litter". He seemed happy to have him just the same. As "Applejack" grew older and much larger, you hardly ever saw Mr. Oscar without him.

According to custom, time passed and life went on.

Although our family couldn't have been framed as a perfectly painted picture, we were family, regardless. Overtime, our picture became one with less eraser marks, smears and smudges, coloring outside of the lines, and fewer things that you can see, but can't understand.

With time, I came to understand that families help one another like Aunt Rita did when Mama got sick; like Papa and Uncle Larry did when Mr. Oscar, the Egg Man accidently struck It. Real families aren't about perfectly painted pictures. They are about love and commitment and trust and unity along with all of the other traits that structure a family. Therefore, family units shouldn't combust or decompose during seasons of inopportunity, but they should continue to love their way through the difficulties.

Many families are guilty of comparing and/or evaluating themselves by another families' plumb line. Each and every unit is as diverse and unique as the individuals within the unit. There are so many different aspects involved in the makeup of the family. It is unwise to judge the status or condition of ourselves or our family unit by that of an individual or family across the street, around the corner, on the television screen or in a magazine.

We fail to mete out true justice to ourselves when our perception of perfect is based upon improper, incomplete, inadequate, or misleading data. Most families only allow us to see the "for public viewing only" picture. Therefore, the information we're trying to process is faulty from the beginning. We don't hang stained or torn garments out in full view. Usually, those garments are not exposed to the public.

Generally, families keep their unflattering characteristics close to the cuff. When there's a breakdown within the family structure, rarely does it get broadcast to the world unless it becomes news and/or gossip, and wisely so. On occasions when one family member's dirty laundry gets willfully aired out in public by another family member, it's seldom, if ever done out of love.

Yet, for one reason or another, we frequently wish that we were born into a different family. However, different means different things to different people: Just as normal and perfect lies in the eyes of the beholder. In some instances, different may mean more loving, less friction, more settled, more stable, more money, etc., but it's never going to mean trouble-free.

A beautifully wrapped box doesn't define the gift that's hopefully inside. Standing on the outside looking in, our vision is obscured. We're viewing only a silhouette, a shadow of reality, and our conclusions are based upon our perception or our fantasy of how perfect or good or happy or strong or affluent is evidenced in our own minds and through our own eyes.

While my family was going through our toughest times, I envisioned myself in another family. From the outside, they appeared to be so happy, so problem-free, so picture perfect. Everyone and every family have issues. They run the gamut from minor to mediocre, from severe to extreme, and in between.

Unfortunately, the issues surrounding this particular family were of a very serious nature, and in the long haul proved to be both painful and disappointing to all involved. That allowed me to see early on: If I didn't want my problems, I definitely didn't want to wish the problems of others upon me. In the words of my Grandma, "I would've been jumping out of a pot full of boiling water into a frying pan full of hot grease".

If we aren't mindful, we can get caught up into a whirlwind of dysfunction. My brother, Alex and I remain close. We are siblings. We are friends. We love and want the best for one another. There are many factors that cause us to be congruent. Howbeit, our individuality and gender differences allow us to frequently have opposing viewpoints. Nonetheless, we're still family. We can disagree, have disagreed, and continued to love each other. One factor doesn't negate the other.

Although we were reared in the same house, had the same parents, endured some of the same struggles, and were feed the same meat and potatoes, we grew up at our own pace, developed our own likes and dislikes, and we also have our very own idiosyncrasies and uniqueness that makes us who we are; separately. Therefore, we have to make a concerted effort to walk continuously in harmonious fellowship.

We have found that additions to the mix tend to change the amount of effort it takes. The congruency of the relationship has been redefined. Marriage and parenthood has shifted our relationship to a degree. Priorities change. Dynamics change. New memories are made. New challenges are overcome.

I now see us as being units within a unit. Nurturing and strengthening our individual units while helping to keep the base strengthened has to be intentional. Achieving the best results possible takes prayer, planning, and work. We need an objective and an expectation in order to maintain a functional relationship. Rifts can occur easier than most of us would like to think. One of our greatest incentives was and still is: not to duplicate the dysfunction that occurred between Papa and Uncle Larry. It affected all of us, and caused us to miss out on more than we'll ever know.

Great bonds require courage. A bond means that we're in relationship. However, that shouldn't deprive any of us of the right to process information and formulate an opinion even if it's based solely upon our own percepts. Being right or being wrong shouldn't come with a price tag that no one can afford to pay. Bondage means that my right to think for myself and reach my own conclusions has been eliminated, and the only way that we can be in a relationship that's satisfying to you is if I conform my way to yours.

Life is progressive. We are constantly growing and learning, thinking and rethinking. As we mature and experience life even some of our learned behaviors are challenged as well as some of our beliefs. Our views may become more conservative or more liberal. One of the challenges become: How to incorporate our assets and liabilities into the mix, thereby, creating a family structure that is solid enough to stand, yet flexible enough to bend without breaking up and falling apart.

First and foremost, I believe, we need to come to the table understanding that none of us are perfect. Each of us have our share of flaws, vulnerabilities, fears, failures and the like, but we also have strengths, passions, dreams, accomplishments, and other outstanding qualities. The makeup of the family shouldn't be an either/or proposition.

Uncle "Bad Manners" and Aunt "Too Loud" still have a place at the table, however irritating and/or embarrassing their habits may be. Sometimes, it may mean that we may have to put some distance between them and ourselves. Chances are they will always show up at the family reunion. In my opinion, we can't disassociate ourselves from or disown our family members simply because we don't agree with them. Life would be unsettling if we were all carbon copies of one another. Thank God for our diverse human race.

LETTING GO

As I jogged along my favorite path,
I saw a little bird lying helplessly on the ground.
I removed the towel from my neck,
Wrapped the bird with the broken wing very carefully,
The little creature was now safe from element and prey.

I nurtured the bird.
I tended its wounds.
I cared for it fully intending to set it free as soon as it was able.
The bird grew stronger and stronger with each passing week.
Its' broken wing began to heal.
And every morning its' song became sweeter and sweeter to my ears.

The more attached I became the longer I prolonged its release.
I really did not want to see it go,
But I knew the time had come.
And I didn't want to withhold this creature's freedom.

I put aside my feelings, opened the cage, and turned away.
I soon heard the flutter of its wings.
I knew that it was gone,
Soaring high with the wind underneath:
Being all that it was created to be.

CHAPTER FIFTEEN

When we began to appreciate our painted picture, in spite of its' flaws, I envisioned my Grandma smiling. I knew she would've thanked God for her sons finally coming to their senses. But, even more than that: They had set one another free. In the interim, they had set themselves free as well.

Un-forgiveness is akin to having someone else chained to your heart, and encapsulated in your mind. Everywhere you go, there they are. To free them is to free self.

Refusing to forgive or to deliberately withhold forgiveness is to purposefully carry unnecessary weights. Seldom does it affect the other person the way we hope. Un-forgiveness, among other things, is an ineffective weapon of revenge. It can be as harmful as a self-inflicted wound. It's also an encumbrance to our very being, and can influence every aspect of our lives.

After Papa and Uncle Larry's relationship changed for the better, it appeared to settle some other issues within our family. Once their feud ended, the atmosphere seemed to change, the heaviness over us lifted. After the heads began the healing process, the rest of the body could begin the process of healing as well.

Peace which seemed as if it were just a distant memory or something that was a total fantasy and/or completely foreign to us finally came. It not only stepped into our yards, it also came inside of our doors, and visited with us for long periods of time. I kept hoping that it would stay forever, but every now and then trouble would rear its' ugly head again.

Yet, whenever trouble visited us without a pass, a welcome, or a warning, I learned that even in the best of families, sometimes, the picture may get all smeared up and poked full of holes. At those times, we must be mindful that trouble doesn't get too comfortable. We cannot allow nor can we afford for it to take up permanent residence in our homes.

At those times when it appears that all hell has broken loose, and the enemy has been given free rein to reap havoc in our lives, I hold onto the promise that this too shall pass. After all, my present or right now faith is based upon my confidence that whatever I'm hoping for will be manifested in the future. My defense is Jesus Christ, the Living Word of God. My offense is the written Word of God. And my weapon of warfare is prayer.

I may come through the battle bruised, a little smoky, but victorious! Being a Christian does not give us a free pass. Trouble will come. Storms will arise. Nevertheless, whenever I try to imagine going through the storm without having the Lord on my side, I am thankful the more that I don't have to. The battle is not mine anyway. Only the power of our Almighty God is able to stop the enemy in his tracks, and defeat every fiery dart he tries to shoot our way!

We weren't given the ability to hope, love, be courageous, patient and to persevere for nothing. We have to put them into action. Unfortunately, challenges may also accompany them. However, challenges help us to grow. Oftentimes, we don't have a clue as to what we're really made out of or what God can do in us and through us until we are faced with a challenge.

I've gained strength, wisdom, courage and understanding from and during some of my most trying circumstances. Though I may have been tossed about during the process as if I were in a raging storm, I continued to hold onto my faith in Christ, believing, I am more than a conqueror. I am an overcomer. I didn't know how He was going to do it. I didn't know when. I just believed that He would. Eventually, He has,

over and over again, but not always according to the way I thought or hoped. God knows what's best for me. If most of us had our rathers, we would rather not go through the trials, tests, or tribulations of life.
Again, life happens. Rain falls upon the just as well as the unjust.

The situations that arise in our lives often bring or create turmoil. What we see, how we feel, and/or how we react helps to paint a picture for ourselves as well as for others, but may not necessarily tell the full story. We can make it through disappointment, betrayal, and pain. We can eventually find a place of solace in our grief. We can. In spite of what the enemy had in mind, we can make it. With God all things are possible. And with love, time, faith and effort, wounds heal. Believe me, I know it's not that easy to let go. Nonetheless, it's very necessary that we don't allow our discomfort to become our hiding place.

Today, I continue to hope. No longer am I hoping for a perfectly painted picture kind of life. Nor am I hoping for a life void of trouble. Instead, for a life where no one and no thing can come along, selfishly smearing our picture or poking holes into our paper. Every time I need a reminder of how precious and how fragile life, love and family are, I take a good, long look at the portrait hanging in our foyer. I then take a deep breath, and prepare to forge ahead to help make our picture the best that it can be. Like It, the beauty is much deeper than surface issues.

I HAVE BEEN THERE TOO!

"But Jesus,

I'm hurt and I don't know what to do.
I've never known anyone who has had to suffer this much.
No one cares and no one understands."

"I understand." Jesus said.
I have walked on long and dusty roads before;
I have stood alone more than a few times too!
I have had to shed some tears;
I have suffered heartaches and disappointments.
I have been through the valley;
I have also been tossed and turned in the storm."

"But, Jesus"

"And in that place where you now find yourself;
I must tell you, I have been there too.
I have had friends to turn their backs on me;
I have been treated unfairly more times than I care to mention.
I have been lied about, laughed at, and beaten.
Those whom I meant no harm have dragged my good name
through the mud.
So you see, I have been there too."

"But, Jesus"

THE PERFECTLY PAINTED PICTURE

"There is absolutely nothing in your path;
Nothing that you cannot endure:
No sorrow, nor grief,
No amount of ridicule,
No injustice, nor shame,
And certainly no amount of suffering,
That I, Jesus have not been through too.

"When you come to me, with great compassion and understanding,
I will reassure and strengthen you.
I will lift you up and give you rest, for I have been there too.
In return for all that I endured, I came not as an avenger.
I came to save, to heal, and to deliver.

"The Father's peace I give to you.
His message of love is hope for the lost and the brokenhearted.
For God so loved even when man was unlovely;
Even when man went his own way, with his heart far from God,
He loved so much that He sent Me,
The Only Begotten Son to redeem man back to Him.

"Sometimes in life, we give love; we sacrifice ourselves, our time,
And even our substance to others who may or may not accept,
Or appreciate all that we have done for them.
So my child, never forget that I have been there too!" Jesus said.

CHAPTER SIXTEEN

It appears, life is throwing nothing but fast balls and curve balls your way—disappointment, heartache, family dysfunction, financial stress, distress, illness, grief, etc.--- are the only pitches making it across the plate.

"Apparently, I can't catch a break." You tell yourself.

You're hitting at the ball, but you're constantly striking out or the homeruns are so far and few between they don't really feel like victories. And you can't even imagine things getting any better.

So you conclude, it's always going to be like this. You try to rationalize, justify, excuse, blame, and/or deny. You have more questions than answers. In relation to the challenges you face, in your eyes, your portion is more than ample. You feel that your serving is disproportionate to your contributions and expectations.

"It's not fair!" You say.

Life isn't going to allow us to effortlessly stroll from base to base, scoring points. During times of trouble, we can eventually make it to home plate, but in between bases – some things will and must occur. The closer we get to home base, the more frequent and the more intense the struggle will become. But it's at those times that we must remain courageous, diligent and tenacious.

Pertaining to life, you perceive that it has been unjust: every mountain has been insurmountable; every valley unending; every molehill a crater. You feel as if you've been in a place of unrest for so long your past, present and future has become disintegrated. In summary, your concept of life towards you is that it has been unrelenting.

Trying to focus on the positive only draws the negative to the forefront. Thereafter, you find yourself thrashing around in a pool of sorrows or drowning in the cesspools of angrier, doubt, and fear.

THE PERFECTLY PAINTED PICTURE

At this point your only strategy is to just allow the ball to hit you so you will be out of the game. Though you are keenly aware that your strategic plan stems from hopelessness, no other alternative will avail itself to you, and you're tired of waiting for a change or for a resolution to just manifest out of thin air.

Although we may become disconsolate, as difficult as it might be to admit to ourselves, some of our issues are due to wrong choices. In correlation, some of our challenges are of no fault of or choice of our own. They are just a result of life's happenings. Troubles arrive in our lives that are beyond our control: accidents, sudden deaths, victimization, and abandonment.

When tumultuous storms arise in our lives, interrupting our tranquility, the normal or expected flow of things, most often we're caught unaware and ill-prepared. However, we're still left to deal with the residuals, the aftermath. Storms usually leave behind debris; the more intensified the storm, the greater the debris.

What happens when perspective, reality, fantasy, and expectation collide, intertwine or began to war against one another?

Oftentimes, the picture we paint of our situations and circumstances is anything but vivid. It's more like an abstract painting. From our point of view it's very undiscerning and disconcerting.

We try many things in our quest to resolve our issues and alleviate our pain. Many of those solutions make matters worse instead of better. Too often we seek fixes which only numb our pain or help us to forget our issues temporarily. Unfortunately, much too often seeking a spiritual resolution is a last resort.

We unwisely put stock in our own abilities or the advice of friends or the urging of family members. In some instances, the situation has to get chaotic: We're reeking with the effluvium of desperation. The pit we're in seems to be suffocating us. We've used every natural means known to us to escape our struggles. We feel as if we're going down for the last time. Sadly, then and only then will we cry out to the Lord. However our struggles, our pain, and even our fears and doubts are no surprise to God. He sees. He knows. And He cares.

Call upon Him. Trust Him. And surrender your all to Him. Apply the measure of faith you've been given and watch it increase.

There comes a time in our lives when we must seek, believe, and trust God for ourselves. Grandma instructed me in the ways of God, but I had to make the choice to serve Him for myself. I realized that I needed and wanted a personal relationship with Him. Whether I'm in a season of daylight or in a very long, night season, I've never regretted my decision to follow Him.

As in Mama's condition, He will be with you in the midst of the storms even when hospitals, doctors, medication, counselors, and/or surgery, is involved. Fear not; we don't have to suffer in silence or inwardly or act out in bitterness, angrier, frustration, or hopelessness. There's a Balm in Gilead to heal the sick and the hurting. He is awaiting your call. Jesus understands where you are. He loves you and has your best interest at heart.

If you are reading these pages and have not accepted Jesus as your Lord and Savior, I admonish you to do so. You don't have to jump through any hoops or turn flips. There's no requirement that you have the ability to pray eloquently or know how to recite Bible verses. You don't even need to have it all together or wait until the time is right. There is no better time than now: where you are; just as you are.

The God of our creation desires to make you whole. There is a void in us that only He can fill. Allow the Spirit to minister to your spirit, to reach those hurting places, and comfort you whether your pain stems from physical, emotional, or spiritual lack—commit it to the Lord. Trust Him with your whole heart. You haven't done anything that will shock God. Actually, He saw you when you did it; heard you when you said it; knew your thoughts even before you thought them. Yet, He allows all of us free will to make our own choices. He is not a puppet master, who manipulates us into following His will.

He wants us to love and serve Him willingly, freely. He loves us unconditionally: through flaws and failures, disobedience and sin, fears and doubt. As perfect as He is, He will never look down on us for our imperfections. Apart from God, we cannot get "right". Never assume that He will not understand. He really does.

We were created with a purpose, but we must choose who we will serve. No one can make that choice for us. Jesus did not come to condemn. He came bearing gifts: love, salvation, liberty, healing, abundant life, wholeness, peace that surpasses all understanding, joy, faith, victory............

It would be extremely unjust if a doctor listened to, empathized with, thereafter diagnosed his/her patients' ills, then patted them on the back, and sent them on their way without offering any relief or remedy.

TAKE ME HIGHER

Please, take me higher, Lord,
So I can see the Son.
The clouds overhead are gray,
And from my view,
I can't see any rays of hope.

From down here,
I am constantly focused on the trouble before me.
I know that I'm supposed to walk by faith,
But Oh Lord, the heaviness is constricting.
My path is filled with pain and uncertainty.

Oh Lord, take me higher,
I need the grace to make it through.
Hide me in the cloud of Your glory.

It's in You that I live, move, and have my being.
I can't do anything apart from You and Your love.

If I am lifted up,
Your radiant light will illuminate all that surrounds me,
And all that is within me.
Oh Lord, please take me higher.

PRAYER

Father, I come to You in humility, obedience, sincerity, and submission. I come in the Name of Your Son and my Lord and Savior, Jesus Christ Who is the Perfect Picture of Your grace and mercy.

Lord, I thank You for always being there for me. Thank You for strengthening and comforting me when life seems to be overwhelming.

Your love and faithfulness gives me the courage I need to get out of bed, to put one foot before the other, and move when adversity tries to lure me.

Father, my eyes are on You. I take You at Your Word. All authority belongs to You. You are Sovereign. You know all things from beginning to end. You are never perplexed by the issues of life.

All of my help comes from You. You have a plan and a purpose for me. Sometimes, I don't understand why I have to travel a certain path, why some doors are closed, why my strategy produces little fruit even when my intentions are good, or why some relationships sour.

I meditate on Your Word, seek Your face, and wait on Your answer, because I believe You know what's best for me. I trust You with my heart, my life, my plans and the outcome.

Father, all that You have promised, I believe and I receive. I wait in earnest expectation for them to be manifested in my life. You have already given me so much. I will never be able to thank You enough. My family: years ago, I couldn't perceive such blessings. I am truly grateful that my heartache was replaced with joy. Triumph stands boldly where trouble once hovered. You've changed doubt and fear into faith and courage. Thank You over and over again for showing me that I am a victor instead of a victim.

Truly, You give a peace that is beyond all understanding. I've spent so much time worrying and crying and spinning my wheels to no avail, but I had to learn to trust and depend upon You completely.

Lord, You have answered my prayers above and beyond my expectations. Everything I'll ever need, You have the power to give: love, abundant life, wholeness and healing, strength, peace, joy, hope, faith, endurance, security, liberty--- Everything!

Father, I believe Your desire is for Your children to lack nothing. I know that doesn't just apply to material goods, but the things that will enrich our lives beyond the temporal.

Lord, for those things that may not change on this side, I pray for the grace to bear them gracefully. And for all of the times I'm sure to fall short, will You intercede for me as You did for Peter, that I not fail.

I commit my life, my family, my job, and my expectations to Your hands. I know that You have my best interest at heart. I pray for the courage to wait, the faith to walk according to the path that You have laid before me even when I can't see or understand it, and the wisdom to speak Your Word over the lives of my family and every situation that arises. I pray that I apply it to our lives daily and not wait for trouble to back me in a corner. I want to serve You and depend on Your provisions totally.

Father, I know that laying my all before You doesn't mean that I have no responsibilities. You have given me a mind, hands, abilities, gifts and talents. I have to make right choices, glorify

You in all I do, and remain diligent.

I'm not a mistake. You didn't create me haphazardly. You knew me beforehand. You have a purpose for my life. You have determined, ordained, and set into motion times and seasons. Like David, I too would've lost heart, and given up if I had not trusted to see Your goodness while I still have breathe.

I'm available to You Most High, All Wise, and Only Living God. I'm Your child and I count it an honor and a privilege to be a servant in Your Kingdom. I want to be holy, pleasing and acceptable in Your sight.

Lord, I give all praises to You.

Amen.

EPILOGUE

Tonight, as Gerald and I were getting the children settled in bed after a visit with the family, we hugged and kissed them goodnight. Before turning off their lights, we reminded them how much we love them, and what a blessing it is to be their parents. Then we embraced one another.

It was good seeing Mama sitting outside, watching the children play. She and Aunt Rita have themselves a little oasis underneath the oak tree. Marie's youngest seemed to be having himself a ball collecting acorns. Life, even with all of its complexities has a certain and enjoyable element that is so simple. We can become preoccupied with the noisiness of life, yet often neglect the quietness.

At least once a year, we arrange our schedules so all of the family can spend a weekend together. It takes quite a bit of planning and effort on our parts to synchronize schedules and accommodations, but the benefits far outweigh the sacrifices. We haven't given our gathering an official sounding name yet.

I always enjoy spending time with my cousins: Marie, Vanessa, Trina, and Leon. I'm glad that our children are becoming friends as well.

Alex made a speech. I was so proud of him. He's definitely not just a dumb, old boy any longer. Actually, he never was. But what fun would there have been in growing up if sisters and brothers and even cousins couldn't tease one another now and again?

On the first night, we stayed up late, talking. Alex related to me that he and Papa had their very first man to man conversation at our last gathering. He said that it turned out to be more like a lecture, but he appreciated it because he knew that it was done out of love.

"When I told Papa that I had proposed to Priscilla, and we had set a date: First, he asked me if I had spoken to her folks beforehand. Next, he smiled, and asked me if I had gotten down on one knee?
"Yes and yes," I answered.
"Well, I hope you didn't give her a ring outta the cereal box." We both laughed.
"Then he grew very serious. 'Son, if you asked her for her hand in marriage, treat her right. Love her the way she deserves to be loved. Take care of her. You got to be prepared to put her needs before yours. Don't try to mold her into a female version of yourself. The man is the head of the home, that is true, but God gave Eve to Adam as a helpmate; not to become his servant.
" 'Don't try to rob her of her right to speak up. Truth be told, womenfolk can see things in a way that menfolk can't even imagine, and vice versa. God gave the man and the woman their own special qualities. Don't crush her spirit.
" 'Married life ain't lovely-dovey every day, but it's a good life. It takes work. Things just ain't gone fall into place simply because you want them to. I regret to this day how things turned out when y'all were children. I can't go back and change nothing though.
" 'Y'all talk things over. Don't let stuff go. It'll fester on you, and before you know it, you'll have yourself a real mess. When trouble comes, it's gone take the two of you working together. Some folks act like marriage is a game of "tug-a-war".
" 'Don't stand up there, making promises to her and before God if you have no intentions of keeping them. If you can't do

right by her, it's best to let her know now. Son, I only say these things to you because I know that I won't the best teacher. I made mistakes with your Mama and you and Marla.

" 'I'm just grateful that your Mama put up with me, forgave me, and chose to stick it out. Son, I tell you the truth, when your Mama got sick, if you and your sister hadn't been there to help keep me together, I doubt if I would be here today. I didn't think that I could take no more.' "

As I view some of the pictures we took at our family gathering, I don't see perfection nor do I seek it, but I do see love; a love that covers, strengthens, upholds, forgives, heals, and unifies.

This year, at the family gathering, Mama and Papa were introduced to our new bundle of joy. Mama made a fuss over her new grandson as grandmothers so often do. When I laid him in Papa's arms, he looked down at Nathan Philip, smiled, looked up at me, then at his grandson again.

"You did good Puddin' – real good." He said in an almost whisper.

PEACE

The smell of my babies, freshly bathed,

Their toothless smiles,

The glitter in their eyes,

The softness of their skin,

Watching over them while they're asleep,

knowing that they're safe.

Relaxing in the quietness after a long day,

Sipping hot tea,

Eating a slice of homemade cake,

Reading a good book,

Cuddled up in my husband's arms,

Engaged in pleasant conversation,

And a good nights' rest.

Remaining in the black after the month's bills are paid,

The discipline to do the right thing—

Sometimes, the hard way,

And still come out on top.

Contemplating just a portion of what God has given,

Absorbing His graciousness,

Giving thanks,

Understanding the meaning of contentment,

Being blessed above and beyond my expectations.

Passing through a troubled moment or a season,

But coming out the better for it.

Knowing that I am loved,

And being capable of expressing love even when there aren't

any visible

or immediate dividends.

After all is said and done—

In spite of everything—

Still declaring, "Life is good!"

Yet, knowing that God is in my corner is the ultimate peace,

Whatsoever comes or goes—

He is more than able to defend.

Because nothing ever baffles or takes Him by surprise!

OH WHAT PEACE---SWEET PEACE INDEED!

THE PERFECTLY PAINTED PICTURE

ANOTHER STROKE OF THE BRUSH

DOING THE RIGHT THING THE HARD WAY

Laila forced her ears into submission by forcing them to hear what she did not want to hear. She willed her body to remain sitting instead of running over to William – leading with him to stop this foolishness – not to do what he was threatening to do. Her heart pounded inside her chest as if she were about to go into cardiac arrest though she dared it to. Through her tears, coughing and nose blowing, Laila struggled to breath.

Yet, William continued to talk as if his wife of nine years was just sitting on the porch swing, taking in a cool breeze. "I have to do this Lay. There's no other way around it." He said factually.

"William, I promise to do better. I will. I know – I know I can." Laila promised in-between sobs.

"Absolutely"! He said sarcastically. "Why don't I just take your word for it? Again! Woman, do you really take me for a fool?" Laila dabbed her eyes with tissue while trying to keep her eyes on her husband at the same time.

William was not a mean man. In fact, he was quite opposite from the man who now stood before her. His mood had changed after the phone call. She had overheard him saying, "I certainly will take care of it. I'll do it TODAY."

She knew throwing a tantrum and hoping against hope that it would sway him would be futile. This time, it appeared no amount of tears or clutching at her chest or reasoning was able to nudge him from his position.

Laila watched as William acted as though her physical discomfort was not his concern. Neither did he do or say anything to indicate otherwise.

Right in the midst of her coughing and shoulder heaving and shaking like someone struggling through a muscle spasm or worse, William took the scissors out of the utility draw and placed them on the counter.

Laila's sobs grew louder.

William opened the door of the cabinet where they kept the 'everyday' drinking glasses, walked over to the refrigerator where he filled the glass with crushed ice, then water.

Laila thought as she watched, "I dare him. I don't want any water!"

She had planned to say, "No thank you" when he offered it to her, but she didn't have the chance. He leaned against the counter and drank it: right before her.

Clearly, he was playing games with her. However, she was not amused. Actually, she was sort of afraid: not of William, but that she had run out of options and tactics.

Nevertheless, Laila coughed a few times as a reminder to herself and to William of where they were in the game. Although she was no longer as sure of the rules as she had been before. Usually, she could persuade her husband of almost anything at any time. Apparently, not this time.

He was going to do it and soon. She could tell.

William picked up the scissors, reached into his pocket with his other hand to retrieve what was causing him to lose his mind and her so much distress. One by one, he began to cut them up, allowing them to fall to the floor. Each made their own unique sound as they fell upon the ceramic tile.

Point!

Laila shivered as if a cold wind had entered into the room. She continued to watch William and could've sworn that he smirked as he performed his—in her mind – incorrigible deed.

Well, if his aim was to make her suffer, he had mastered his goal. And if he was satisfied, she most certainly was not! William then went to the closet, got the broom and dustpan and began to sweep up the remains. He sighed loudly as if to say, "Now, I can breathe again".

What William had done had been long in the making. Laila knew that her husband seldom denied her, but things were getting out of control, and was affecting their life adversely and unnecessarily. In her heart she knew it, but head and habit was another story.

Still, at this time, she viewed what her husband had done to her credit cards as cruel and unusual punishment. Nonetheless, it was done. Laila felt the need to lie down. The grieving process had begun.

She stood, walked slowly to their room, coughed and dabbed at her tears along the way. Somehow, the hallway seemed longer.

William went out to the garage.

Game over!

THE PERFECTLY PAINTED PICTURE

www.ingramcontent.com/pod-product-compliance
Lightning Source LLC
Chambersburg PA
CBHW071233090426
42736CB00014B/3063